Confronting Cyber Risk

T0331979

Confronting Cyber Risk

An Embedded Endurance Strategy for Cybersecurity

Gregory Falco and Eric Rosenbach

OXFORD
UNIVERSITY PRESS

Oxford University Press is a department of the University of Oxford. It furthers
the University's objective of excellence in research, scholarship, and education
by publishing worldwide. Oxford is a registered trade mark of Oxford University
Press in the UK and certain other countries.

Published in the United States of America by Oxford University Press
198 Madison Avenue, New York, NY 10016, United States of America.

Library of Congress Cataloging-in-Publication Data
Names: Falco, Gregory, author. | Rosenbach, Eric, author.
Title: Confronting cyber risk : an embedded endurance strategy for
cybersecurity / by Gregory Falco and Eric Rosenbach.
Description: New York, NY : Oxford University Press, [2022]
Identifiers: LCCN 2021037378 (print) | LCCN 2021037379 (ebook) |
ISBN 9780197526545 (paperback) | ISBN 9780197526569 (epub) |
ISBN 9780197526576
Subjects: LCSH: Computer security. | Computer networks—Security measures.
| Internet—Security measures. | Risk management.
Classification: LCC QA76.9.A25 F334 2022 (print) | LCC QA76.9.A25 (ebook) |
DDC 005.8—dc23
LC record available at https://lccn.loc.gov/2021037378
LC ebook record available at https://lccn.loc.gov/2021037379

DOI: 10.1093/oso/9780197526545.001.0001

1 3 5 7 9 8 6 4 2

Printed by LSC Communications, United States of America

Contents

Preface

Our digitally dependent world has a problem. Many leaders relegate cyber risk management to technical experts. By making cybersecurity a technical issue, leaders exacerbate the challenge of an already complex problem and increase their organization's risk of being attacked. This book seeks to change that paradigm by providing both a strategy and recommended actions for leaders seeking to address cyber issues in their organizations. In short, this book is a cyber risk leadership guide for all types of non-cyber-experts: the senior executive worried about the scourge of ransomware hitting midsize companies around the world, the general counsel hoping to limit the potential litigation risk of a data breach, even the new network administrator hoping to understand the non-technical aspects of cybersecurity.

The book is centered around a series of core questions addressed in each chapter. While the book can be read cover to cover, it is also digestible in a modular fashion—allowing readers to choose the questions (chapters) that most interest them without requiring knowledge from previous chapters.

The questions are largely strategic in nature, and the subsequent material in each chapter offers both the 10,000-foot view as well as a deeper dive on each topic. They include:

- Why is cyber risk an issue?
- Who is attacking us?
- How do I assess our cyber risk?
- What do I need to know about cyber frameworks, standards, and laws?
- Who is responsible for cybersecurity?
- What risk prevention measures can I use?
- What risk resilience measures can I use?

- How do I embed cyber risk management in all aspects of the organization?

Each chapter contains six sections, which are designed to be independently readable. These are:

- Case Study—a real-world illustration of the topic at hand
- Why It Matters—the motivation for learning the chapter's content
- Key Concepts—the ideas foundational to answering the chapter's question
- Going Deeper—what the experts know
- Taking Action—how you can act on what you've just learned
- Main Takeaway—the Big Idea you carry to the next board meeting, strategy session, or water-cooler chat

The cases are not intended to serve as comprehensive summaries of incidents. Rather, each case represents the essence of the chapter's challenge. Some cases describe incidents that occurred several years ago, while others are more recent. The older cases are as important as those that have captured recent headlines, since they have stood the test of time by exemplifying what *not* to do or how things can go wrong.

We have selected these cases and structured this book based on decades of combined practical experience developing and running cyber-resilient organizations in both the private and public sectors. We are confident the book's content and design will empower you to get the answers you need, and thus better enable your organization to navigate a treacherous cyber threat and risk landscape.

This book is derived from work that we jointly completed for the HarvardX online course Cybersecurity: Managing Risk in the Information Age. We appreciate all the contributions from students, colleagues, and industry experts as we honed the Embedded Endurance strategy. We also would like to thank the tutors and GetSmarter team that help make the course a success.

We would also like to acknowledge that this material was licensed for publication courtesy of the President and Fellows of Harvard College.

We could not have completed this book without the tireless efforts of Cameron Hickert. Hickert was instrumental in shaping and writing the case studies, cryptograms, and overall context of the book. Hickert is among the top 1 percent of talent at Harvard University and is one of the most motivated and strategic critical thinkers that we have had the opportunity to work with in our respective roles across government, industry, and academia. As Hickert redefines the technology landscape through his AI research and development while engaging in political strategy formulation relating to China and other U.S. competitors across the digital landscape, we are certain he will emerge as a future leader in both industry and government.

1
Why Is Cyber Risk an Issue?

The importance of understanding and managing cyber risk for the organization

Case Study

On a Friday in May 2017, a North Korean cyberattack dubbed "WannaCry" gripped the globe.[1] In the first few hours, 70,000 machines worldwide were infected.[2] Only two days later, that number had ballooned to 200,000.[3] The figure would have risen even higher, but a British cybersecurity researcher chanced upon a "kill switch" that crippled the attack.[4]

How It Happened

WannaCry was a form of ransomware. Upon infection, it encrypted a computer's files, holding them hostage in the hopes of extracting a ransom from the user. Fortunately, before the attack, engineers had already released a software update inoculating computers against WannaCry. However, many organizations failed to apply the patch.[5]

The Impact

The worm's final toll was immense: over 230,000 machines infected across more than 150 countries, tallying over $4 billion in losses.

Confronting Cyber Risk. Gregory Falco and Eric Rosenbach, Oxford University Press. © Oxford University Press 2022. DOI: 10.1093/oso/9780197526545.003.0001

Organizations as diverse as FedEx,[6] Taiwan Semiconductor Manufacturing Co.,[7] the University of Montreal,[8] and Honda experienced significant operational outages.[9]

Particularly hard hit was the United Kingdom's National Health Service (NHS). In all, the WannaCry attack cost the NHS more than $100 million.[10] More than one in three trusts (the fundamental organizational units of the NHS) faced disruption due to the attack, nearly 20,000 appointments or operations were canceled, and multiple emergency departments were forced to divert patients elsewhere.[11]

Behind the Scenes

WannaCry did not specifically target the NHS, so what led to this dramatic impact? Two failures stand out.

The NHS's first misstep was its cyber risk assessment process—more specifically, its response to previous assessments. Reaching as far back as three years before WannaCry, the United Kingdom's Department of Health and Social Care had warned NHS trusts to migrate from old software. In the weeks just preceding the attack, NHS Digital (which runs information technology for the healthcare system) again warned trusts to apply the patch that would have prevented WannaCry from infiltrating their machines.[12] But a report from the country's national auditor found that the department "had no formal mechanism for assessing whether NHS organizations had complied with its advice and guidance."[13]

Consequently, these updates fell by the wayside. In fact, only two-thirds of the trusts had patched their systems before WannaCry.[14] Moreover, when NHS Digital evaluated cybersecurity at eighty-eight trusts—a pool representing one-third of all trusts—prior to the attack, not a single one passed the assessment.[15]

The NHS's second failure was its lack of an effective cyber crisis plan. A Parliament report concluded that the system "had not shared and tested plans for responding to a cyber attack."[16]

Such a strategy should include technical details, but the WannaCry chaos also exposed defects in the NHS's people management. No formal backup communication system replaced the disabled email systems at various trusts. Instead, local NHS organizations resorted to an amalgam of mobile phones, WhatsApp, and pen and paper to transmit and record information.[17,18] And, unsure of where to turn during the crisis, local NHS trusts contacted a hodgepodge of national and local bodies—even local police forces—to report the attack.[19]

These errors are manifestations of a deeper issue: the NHS failed to understand cyber risk as a systemic risk, both within individual trusts and across the national network. Still, as the Parliament report put it, "the NHS was lucky." Beyond the fortuitous kill-switch discovery, the attack's timing—on a summer Friday afternoon—helped the organization dodge an even greater disaster.

Learning to Do Better

The case study of WannaCry and the NHS's response hints at an answer to the question "Why is cyber risk an issue?" This chapter will explore this topic and introduce the key components of today's cyber landscape, in addition to explaining the necessity of adopting a systemic view of cyber risk. It will sketch the outlines of a successful cyber risk management approach that all readers can apply to the cybersecurity needs of their organization.

Why It Matters

In 1951, the Lyons Electronic Office I (LEO I) was introduced as the world's first commercial computer. Initially used for administrative duties such as payroll and inventory record-keeping, it signified a groundbreaking step in the integration of computer systems with business processes. Seven decades later, it is difficult to conceive of any sphere of everyday life that isn't affected by the influence of computing technology. Moreover, computers are no longer the freestanding systems they were only twenty years ago. Whether embedded in a smartphone, a laptop, an office printer, or a car, almost every computer is part of an interconnected web of devices.

Interconnectivity comes at a cost. Rapid growth in the digital environment has created gaps in organizations' cybersecurity awareness, making it easy for threat actors, such as nation-states and cybercriminals, to exploit widely known vulnerabilities. Consequently, cyber risk management, which is the process of preventing cyberattacks and maximizing organizational resilience to them, has developed into an essential requirement for senior executives and key leaders responsible for operations.[20]

The interconnectivity of the numerous parties relying on the internet to achieve various purposes has created a diverse cyber threat landscape. All entities, whether individuals, privately owned companies, or governmental organizations, must deal with the constant threat of cyberattacks. While many organizations believe that implementing robust cybersecurity measures is enough to protect their information systems from hackers, it is inevitable that all beneficiaries of the internet will have to confront cyberattacks at some point.[21]

Cyber risk management is broken. Today we live in a world of cyber "haves" and "have-nots." The "haves" spend millions of dollars on the latest technical defenses to improve the perception of their organization's security. Most of these defenses are Band-Aids. Those organizations in the "have-not" category wait for a disaster and then try to pick up the pieces. Neither approach is sustainable. You need a strategy and you need to take action.

Key Concepts

1. Cyber risk defined
2. Cyber risk management
3. Embedded Endurance: a cyber risk strategy

Cyber Risk Defined

Although it is impossible to fully predict where and when an attack might occur, any cyber risk strategy must start with a clear-eyed assessment of areas that require improved resource allocation.[22] In this context, risk is defined as the product of threats, vulnerabilities, and impact, divided by mitigations.

$$\text{Risk} = \frac{\text{Threats} \times \text{Vulnerabilities} \times \text{Impact}}{\text{Mitigations}}.$$

Each of these components is defined here.

1. **Threats:** Your organization needs to consider any sources of intentional threats that could have a potentially negative impact on its assets. These intentional threats include insiders, cybercriminals, and nation-states.[23]
2. **Vulnerabilities:** Threats rely on vulnerabilities to undermine an organization's cybersecurity, so it is crucial that the most significant vulnerabilities are identified and considered. Vulnerabilities could take the form of poor business processes, poorly educated employees, or outdated software.[24]
3. **Impact:** Your organization must take the potential impact of a cyberattack into account. Assessing the potential impact of a cyberattack involves understanding the effects that various threat scenarios could lead to. For example, an organization could assess the potential impact that a distributed denial-of-service attack (an attack that restricts available bandwidth by flooding networks with unmanageable amounts of data) could have on its system, and how a critical failure of that system would affect critical business operations.[25]
4. **Mitigations:** As your organization takes steps to reduce threats, vulnerabilities, and their impact, it is important to account for these as part of your risk posture. Some mitigation activities are focused on addressing just one aspect of risk, whereas other mitigations are systemic and address each risk consideration across an organization.

Note that this definition of risk has one prerequisite: first you must identify all the assets that constitute your organization. This includes all physical or digital components such as computers, data, and intellectual property.[26]

There are three principal risk categories that an organization could face in the event of a cybersecurity incident:[27]

1. **Business operational risk:** The potential for direct or indirect loss that results from the failure of key business systems, processes, procedures, or people.
2. **Reputational risk:** The potential for loss or damage that results from harm caused to an organization's reputation or public image.
3. **Legal and compliance risk:** The potential for loss or damage that results from legal action being taken against an organization for breaching the law or regulatory requirements.

Cyber Risk Management

The traditional approach to cybersecurity generally focuses on designing a defensive perimeter and network that attempt to prevent valuable assets from being hacked. This approach is based on an informed understanding of potential cyber threats to the organization. Although preventative approaches are crucial for securing assets from conventional methods of attack, stopping there results in an organization that has not truly prepared for the impact of a successful attack.

Rather than pursuing a simplistic security-focused strategy, modern organizations take a risk management approach to cyber. Risk management is the process of identifying risk, assessing risk, and taking steps to reduce risk to an acceptable level.[28] Cyber risk management strategies foster cyber strength by considering critical business processes and allocating more resources to risk resilience, while also emphasizing the implementation of preventative technical cybersecurity mechanisms to protect assets from cyber threats.[29]

As can be seen in the WannaCry case study, individual organizations' cyber susceptibility can cause impacts well beyond their own organization. During the WannaCry attack, information technology failures within individual NHS trusts contributed to communication failures within those trusts, and ultimately to communication failures between trusts. Beyond the NHS trusts directly impacted by the ransomware, their cyber issues resulted in stress to their organization's ecosystem of nearby civic systems and people, such as the police, who were inundated with calls for support during WannaCry. Globally, WannaCry spread from organization to organization; just as one person's illness can spread from organ to organ or to other people, one organization's cyber risk can increase the operational risk for other organizational components or for other organizations within the same ecosystem. For example, major ransomware attacks like WannaCry have disrupted many organizations' global supply chains, which has resulted in the organizations' inability to deliver goods and services. By adopting an Embedded Endurance strategy, digital assets and the organization overall will be buffered from some of the interdependent impacts of cyber risk, enabling sustained mission resilience.

Embedded Endurance: A Cyber Risk Strategy

Addressing cyber risk is a highly interdisciplinary challenge that requires the cooperation of stakeholders with diverse backgrounds.[30] This is reflected in industry, government, and even academia. It is not always clear where one realm of expertise ends and another begins, which necessitates strong leadership that can play the role of traffic controller across the various parts of an organization that address cyber risk. For example, who gets to make the call that the ransom being demanded by attackers should be negotiated and paid? A range of senior-ranking executives and officials will help to make these decisions, but often there are ego issues and multiple stakeholders to consider, so at the end of the day this engagement will not be successful without a strong leadership strategy.

Based on our decades of experience in the real-world trenches of cybersecurity and on research at Harvard, we developed a new strategy called Embedded Endurance. Embedded Endurance is a risk management strategy that applies preventative and resilience measures across the organization both holistically and at the component level to enable sustained mission success in light of persistent threats. The notion of *embeddedness* speaks to the component-level and interdependent nature of each digital asset and its cyber risk, where organizations are a "system of systems"—not unlike how the human body is an organism composed of many organs that work in concert. *Endurance* describes the need for sustainable operations of the system as a whole even in the face of inevitable threats over the long term. Embedded Endurance emphasizes the need to address attack prevention and the resilience of each digital asset while also accounting for the impact on the system's overall operations.

An Embedded Endurance strategy embraces the reality of interdependent digital assets and provides an approach that addresses cyber risk management at both the micro level (people, networks, systems, and data) and the macro level (the organization). As part of an Embedded Endurance strategy, organizations address cyber risk as a systemic concern across interdependent ecosystems of organizations. Utilizing Embedded Endurance helps to reduce the shock waves across the overall system when one digital asset is impacted.

The Embedded Endurance cyber risk management strategy focuses on developing mitigation measures that minimize cyber vulnerabilities and maximize an organization's ability to respond to cyberattacks. There are two types of mitigation measures: prevention and resilience.

- **Prevention measures** engage directly with the vulnerabilities that cause risk to actively ensure that harm does not occur. This engagement often takes the form of threat intelligence, information sharing, and tools that can be employed to limit the interaction of threats with your organization.

- **Resilience measures** focus on bolstering the organization so that regardless of the impact of cyber incidents, the organization can continue operations and achieve its mission.

Cybersecurity is a multidimensional issue that requires organizations to take several variables into account to ensure that their information systems remain resilient to potential cyberattacks. An Embedded Endurance approach to cyber risk management should thus consider technical, human, and physical factors when securing systems, networks, and data.[31]

Technical Considerations

Technical considerations include all the tools and processes that protect the devices that could act as a potential entry point for unauthorized access to information systems.[32] For example, due to rapid advancements in the Internet of Things (IoT), organizations must now consider the security of all conventional work-related devices connected throughout their networks, such as mobile devices and printers, as well as seemingly innocuous devices such as thermostats and electronic door locks.

Human Considerations

Human considerations include issues of governance, as described previously, as well as providing employee awareness training and fostering a culture of cybersecurity. Over the past decade, the scope of cyberattacks has expanded to reach far outside of the cyber dimension of information security. Although tools (in the form of software) exist to protect the devices that constitute an organization's digital assets, many cyberattacks infiltrate systems through the users who have access to those assets.

It is therefore important that organizations equip their employees to recognize the types of social engineering attacks (such as phishing emails) that take advantage of human error and negligence. This can be achieved through awareness programs and the fostering of a company-wide culture that emphasizes the value of cybersecurity.

Physical Considerations

In cybersecurity, physical considerations should complement technical and human considerations. Attackers often take advantage of physical access to information systems to execute their hacking activities. To do so, they may leverage poor physical access controls to facilities that house important digital components, or rely on social engineering techniques that trick users into granting hackers physical access to information systems.

Going Deeper

Investment Growth in Information Technology and Operational Technology

To remain competitive, both private and public organizations have invested in information technology (IT), financial technology (fintech), and operational technology (OT) to improve the speed and efficiency of their operations. An organization's IT environment consists of hardware, software, and network resources, which may be housed within the organization's facilities or based on a cloud service hosted by an external entity. Operational technology refers to digital systems that have both cyber and physical implications, such as smart meters, autonomous vehicles, and a variety of control systems that are digitally controlled but have physical impacts on their environment. Financial technology often has elements of both IT and OT systems. Interest in fintech has exploded in recent years given the growth of e-commerce platforms and the need for various financial mechanisms to enable these transactions, such as mobile payments. As the world continues the rapid transition to cashless, digital forms of payment, the risk to both individual organizations and the global economic ecosystem will increase.

Investing in these technologies benefits organizations in the following ways:

- **Increased profitability:** Profitability relies heavily on the efficiency of an organization's processes. IT infrastructure provides managers with the tools and devices necessary to optimize critical business processes, allowing for improved profits over time and greater accessibility to information. OT can facilitate automation of business functions, which also can drastically increase the efficiency of an organization.
- **Improved customer service:** With IT infrastructure, businesses have easier access to customers' information, allowing them to tailor their offerings to their customers' needs. Furthermore, improved access to inventory management data can reduce response time and resolve lingering back-order issues. OT helps to provide seamless experiences for customers by enabling consistent control over certain functions.
- **Efficient internal controls and communication:** By centralizing information storage and controls, organizations can improve their oversight and actuation of the controls responsible for preventing and detecting operational issues. This allows for expedient feedback, which reduces the chances of harm to business operations or assets in the event of an unanticipated situation.

The Link Between Digital Infrastructure and Cyber Risk

While investing in information and operational technology is often an efficient response to the need for optimizing business processes and responding to customer demand, the WannaCry case study illustrates how this also exposes organizations to accompanying cyber threats with the potential to cause large-scale damage. This exposure has the added effect of increasing the variety of targets—what is commonly referred to in cybersecurity terms as the "surface area"—for threat actors, who have a variety of motivations and employ ever more complex methods of attack.[33]

Given the multitude of threats in the current cyber threat landscape, it is important to keep in mind that cyberattacks have one thing in common: they are asymmetric in nature. This means hackers face relatively low risk and could gain disproportionately large rewards, whereas the defender often faces high risk and an impossibly large surface area to protect. Today, businesses cannot fully protect themselves from cyberattacks. This is why cyber risk management's resilience tools are so essential.

Cyberattacks Connecting the Cyber and Physical Dimensions

Although the effects of cyberattacks are generally considered to be limited to information assets, the use of cyber-physical systems (physical systems that are integrated with online systems) has allowed the impact of cyberattacks to cross over from the digital to the physical sphere.[34] The Internet of Things (IoT) refers to physical devices that are augmented with sensory technologies (such as smart thermostats), communications (such as Alexa and other smart speakers), and information-storing technologies (such as Favorite locations on your car's GPS). These smart devices are designed to provide opportunities for integrating the physical world with the cyber world, thereby creating efficient services and processes that require minimal human influence.[35]

The drive to create smart devices has illuminated the fact that any vulnerabilities in devices connected to the Internet of Things could potentially be breached and exploited, leaving targeted devices open to criminal activity, and possible physical manipulation.[36] There are various security concerns with IoT devices ranging from weak password authentication to generally bug-ridden and vulnerable software.

Taking Action

Given the complex and ever-changing nature of the cyber land-scape, it is difficult to pinpoint a single risk management lever that can appropriately address all the vulnerabilities of a business's digital systems. Embedded Endurance provides a steadfast cyber strategy for each business process. The most concrete action you can take to improve your organization's cyber risk management starts with distributing and assigning responsibility for cyber risk.

Distributing and Assigning Leadership Responsibility for Cyber Risk

Organizations need to ensure that each stakeholder is aware of his or her role in maintaining cybersecurity processes and policies.[37]

- **Every member of the organization:** For a cyber risk strategy to be successful, every member of an organization must have a clearly defined role to play in protecting its critical systems, networks, and data. Outside of the reporting structure, cybersecurity should be considered a cultural value shared throughout an organization, rather than a technical process headed by a handful of actors.[38] Most attacks take the form of malware and phishing, which are methods of intrusion that thrive on the negligence and mistakes of those they target.[39]
- **Executive members:** Executives need not become experts in the technicalities of cybersecurity, but it is important to distribute the responsibility for cybersecurity beyond the chief information officer (CIO) or the chief information security officer (CISO). In particular, the chief executive officer (CEO) needs to be ultimately accountable for cybersecurity, and the board of directors must ensure that he or she is executing on this portfolio.
- **Risk committee:** An emergent practice is for organizations to establish a risk committee comprising board members,

representatives from various departments (e.g., legal, human resources, physical security, and cybersecurity teams), and members of the executive management team (CEO, CISO, general counsel, chief risk officer, etc.). The risk committee is empowered to follow the reporting line up to the level of an organization's board members, ensuring that issues of cybersecurity are resolved in a timely manner.[40]

- **CEO:** As mentioned previously, the CEO is ultimately responsible for the organization's cybersecurity. One key component of this function is to execute the cybersecurity strategy advised by the risk committee. As the CEO and board of directors are responsible for an organization's performance, they also have a fiduciary duty to ensure that their organization's cybersecurity is effectively managed. The CEO sets the tone for cybersecurity by making it an important part of the organizational culture.

Action on the Front Lines

This chapter's case study illustrated the dangers that arise when an organization fails to adequately account for cyber risk. NHS leadership could have prevented WannaCry's infiltration of their systems by following through on guidance issued after previous assessments. The organization could have boosted its resilience had NHS leaders created and stress-tested cyberattack response plans. Both of these would have improved the health system's Embedded Endurance.

Throughout our careers, we've consistently heard leaders ask, "What are the most important things I need to do to protect my organization from cyberattacks?" For Rosenbach, the most indelible memory came during a tense meeting in the conference room of the U.S. secretary of defense, when the secretary was excoriating the seniormost members of the military for lax cybersecurity after a penetration of their networks. Afterward, those same leaders came to Rosenbach to ask for the title of *the* leadership book on cybersecurity issues—which, unfortunately, did not exist.

For Falco, the defining moment that called for a comprehensive but realistic cyber risk strategy guide took place in a boardroom where he was advising senior telecommunications, utility, and city government leadership on their smart-city program. Contrary to guidance, they decided that their cyber risk strategy for the multibillion-dollar digital infrastructure overhaul would be . . . encryption. Of course encryption is helpful, but no single technology, tool, or process alone makes for a *strategy*.

One important aspect of leadership comprises the actions taken to mobilize a team to create and execute a goal-driven strategy. The four-star military officers realized that if the security of their networks and data was important to the secretary of defense, it was a *leadership issue*.

Main Takeaway

Mitigating the cyber risk to your organization is an important leadership issue that requires a carefully crafted strategy. Connected information systems provide vast opportunities for organizations to improve the efficiency of key business processes by integrating those processes with an online information infrastructure. However, the constant presence of threats creates cyber risk.

The Embedded Endurance cyber risk management strategy focuses on developing mitigation measures that minimize cyber vulnerabilities and maximize an organization's ability to respond to cyberattacks. There are two types of mitigation measures: prevention and resilience.

2

Who Is Attacking Us?

An overview of threat actors and their motivations for attacking

Case Study

Were Joseph Blount involved in a different line of work, perhaps he could have suffered his company's ransomware attack in relative anonymity. But as CEO of Colonial Pipeline, a company that provides gasoline and oil to more than 50 million Americans, hiding was not an option.[1]

"We were perfectly happy having no one know who Colonial Pipeline was, and unfortunately that's not the case anymore," he summarized. "Everybody in the world knows."[2]

What Happened?

On a Friday in May 2021, Blount discovered his company had been breached.[3] The attack stunned control room employees with the classic ransomware threat: pay up, or else.[4]

In this case, the "or else" was a double threat. The day before they locked Colonial's systems, the hackers had stolen over 100 gigabytes of the company's data.[5] Now they not only wanted Blount's organization to pay a price for the key to resume system operations, but also wanted a fee in exchange for deleting—rather than leaking—the stolen data.[6]

Confronting Cyber Risk. Gregory Falco and Eric Rosenbach, Oxford University Press. © Oxford University Press 2022. DOI: 10.1093/oso/9780197526545.003.0002

The hack had not directly targeted the company's operational networks, instead focusing on its business networks.[7] Still, Colonial had little choice but to shut down pipeline operations in an effort to diagnose and contain the damage—not to mention the fact that Blount's team could no longer track distribution or bill customers.[8]

Many cybersecurity experts hate to see victims pay up; after all, if no one paid, ransomware hackers would not have any incentive to strike. Those who pay often do so in secret to avoid public scrutiny; this, in turn, adds a further barb to the hackers' threat to leak data, as the release doubles as a public shaming. Others argue there is merit to prioritizing your organization's needs and negotiating with the attackers—a form of defensive social engineering.[9] In admitting his decision to pay the $4.4 million ransom (sent to the hackers via cryptocurrency), Blount acknowledged, "I know that's a highly controversial decision. . . . I wasn't comfortable seeing money go out the door to people like this."[10]

The Impact

The shutdown made national headlines instantly. Colonial's 5,500-mile network spans from the Gulf Coast to the Northeast and moves more than 100 million gallons of petroleum product daily.[11] This amounts to almost half of all the fuel that the East Coast consumes.[12]

The pipeline remained offline for five days, and it was not until the following Monday—ten days in total—that Colonial reported throughput was back to normal levels.[13] Despite a company history of more than fifty years and critical infrastructure that routinely experiences hurricanes, never before had the pipeline been entirely shut down.[14]

Making matters worse, news of the attack triggered a run on gasoline, and over 12,000 gas stations across more than ten states went dry.[15] At points nearly one in every two gas stations in Georgia, South Carolina, and Virginia were without fuel;[16] the proportion of empty stations in North Carolina reached above seven in ten.[17]

In addition to the multimillion-dollar ransom, the attack cost Blount's company tens of millions in lost productivity and restoration costs.[18] It also attracted the government's eye; within two weeks the U.S. House Committee on Homeland Security announced that Blount would testify at a hearing on the cyberattack.

Who Did It?

In the week following the attack, the FBI cut short speculation about its origins by attributing responsibility to the DarkSide ransomware group.[19]

Despite appearing less than a year before its attack on Colonial Pipeline, DarkSide had already made a name for itself as a leader in the surging world of ransomware. The criminal group—believed to have been based in the former Soviet bloc—claimed to have hacked more than eighty companies.[20] In the first quarter of 2021 alone the group brought in at least $46 million.[21]

DarkSide operated as a ransomware-as-a-service platform, offering malware and other tools to affiliated hackers for a slice of their earnings.[22] A defining feature was its professionalization of ransomware operations; services ranged from providing tech support to issuing press releases.[23] It claimed a rulebook that forbade attacks on organizations such as hospitals (a popular ransomware target) and schools, and even donated to charities in an attempt to boost its profile.[24]

Blount might have found small solace in the fact that the publicity contributing to his headaches also frustrated DarkSide. As the attack's effects cascaded across state borders, the group vowed to "introduce moderation and check each company that our partners want to encrypt to avoid social consequences in the future."[25]

Citing international law enforcement pressure, the group ultimately announced it had lost access to its infrastructure and claimed to be shutting down (perhaps as an attempt to escape the limelight).[26] Regardless of the status of the DarkSide brand, the broader ransomware industry it represented remains a significant and growing threat to organizations worldwide.

This chapter tackles the question Blount asked as he surveyed his immobilized systems, and one that leadership of all organizations should ask before disaster strikes: "Who is trying to attack us?" The coming pages will explain different types of cyberattacks, detail the suite of actors who launch them, and identify the dominant attacks in specific industries.

Why It Matters

In order to prepare for the inevitability of a cyberattack, organizations need to understand the methods of attack that attackers are likely to utilize in attempts to defeat their cybersecurity.

The concepts discussed in these pages provide a foundational understanding of the prominent forms of malware and cyberattacks that organizations face, and who launches such attacks. The information explored here will equip you to interpret how a hack works, and thus understand how to use an Embedded Endurance strategy in your organization through the appropriate prevention and resilience mitigation measures.

Key Concepts

1. Threat actors
2. Types of attacks
3. Malware

Threat Actors

Cyber threat actors are the cause of cyber risk. Cyber threats are typically defined as anything that can cause damage or loss by exploiting vulnerabilities in an organization's information systems.[27] They are generally perceived as malicious acts—for example, a hacker's deliberate attempt to undermine an organization's cybersecurity measures to access critical information or systems. However, unintentional acts—such as those caused by human error—can also pose considerable risk, even though they are not deliberate attempts to undermine security.[28]

In addition to classification by intent, cyber threats can be further categorized according to source; they can originate from outside an organization (external sources) or from inside (internal sources).[29] These classifications ultimately yield four types of threats: malicious external, malicious internal, unintentional external, and unintentional internal.[30]

As the cyber threat landscape evolves, the types of threat actors grow increasingly diverse. Threat actors range from opportunistic hackers who are merely after bragging rights to highly skilled, nation-state-backed teams who launch sophisticated cyberattacks over prolonged periods of time. Effective risk mitigation thus relies heavily on identifying the types of threat actors that are most likely to attack your organization's information systems, as well as understanding the methods they are likely to use.

Types of Attacks

Methods of cyberattacks can differ based on the intentions of the hackers who utilize them.

Social Engineering

Social engineering techniques rely on psychological maneuvering to trick individuals into downloading malicious software or into unwittingly assisting hackers with cyberattacks. Following are various ways in which hackers achieve this:

- **Phishing:** links that redirect users to dummy websites masked as legitimate web pages, where users are prompted to share confidential information or to complete a certain activity, such as downloading a file[31]
- **Spear phishing:** personalized attack that targets specific individuals

- **Baiting:** strategically leaving infected flash drives in places where targeted users are likely to find them, plug them in, and thereby download malicious software[32]
- **Quid pro quo:** impersonating IT staff, requesting login details or direct access to an organization's information system under the pretense of needing to install software or perform updates[33]
- **Tailgating:** gaining physical access to the targeted company's facilities by simply waiting for authorized individuals to open the door and then walking in behind them[34]

Denial-of-Service Attacks

A denial-of-service (DoS) attack attempts to render a system inoperable by flooding it with more traffic or data than its server can manage. Often these attacks involve hackers installing malware on multiple computers—which makes for a distributed denial-of-service (DDoS) attack—that then form part of the hacker's botnet. A botnet, also referred to as a "zombie army," describes a group of computers that are infected with malware allowing them to be controlled remotely. The malware allows hackers to use the infected computers to overwhelm a targeted system's networks. This is achieved by linking all infected computers that form part of the hacker's botnet to a single controller. The controller prompts each of the infected computers to direct data through the system's network until the amount of data becomes unmanageable and the network loses functionality. This overload of the targeted system's networks disrupts the server's usual services or makes it nearly impossible to access the server's web pages.

Advanced Persistent Threats

An advanced persistent threat (APT) is a sophisticated cyberattack that uses multiple phases to stealthily gain unauthorized access to a network to extract as much data as possible over a prolonged period. Many APT attackers pursue their objectives over months or years. APTs are considerably more complex than the attacks mentioned previously, often incorporating a number of different types of attacks to ensure that hackers can infiltrate a system while remaining undetected throughout all stages of the attack. This allows the hackers, who often function as a team, to extract as much information as possible. APT attacks require considerably more resources than other forms of cyberattack, which is why they are most often carried out by nation-states.

Brute-Force Attacks

A brute-force attack is a method that uses trial and error to eventually guess the correct password necessary to gain access to a system. As this is an exceedingly time-consuming method, hackers generally rely on software to systematically comb through all possible passwords until the correct one is found.

Attacks on AI Systems

As novel artificial intelligence (AI) technologies proliferate, so does the possibility for attacks against them. In addition to the "traditional" types of cyberattacks, adversaries have two additional means of attacking these systems. First, the AI algorithms themselves may have inherent weaknesses that attackers can exploit to surprising effect. In one famous example, researchers found they could fool an AI vision system into ignoring stop signs just by placing a few playing-card-sized stickers on them that a human driver would barely register.[35] Second, modern AI systems are heavily dependent upon the data they learn from, and thus attackers can delete or alter the data to disrupt the system—as one AI phrase summarizes, "Garbage in, garbage out." But beware: we often find that AI practitioners worry so much about these new attack types that they fail to secure their systems against less novel methods.

Malware

As organizations develop increasingly robust resilience to the unpredictability of the cyber landscape, cybercriminals respond by employing more sophisticated methods of cyberattack. The various types of attacks described generally require the installation of malicious code, known as malware, on a targeted system. "Malware" is a term that encompasses various types of malicious software specifically designed to exploit vulnerabilities and flaws in program code, allowing the hacker to attack other forms of software and cause them to behave in unintended or harmful ways. Once malware has been installed, hackers may use the malicious software to steal sensitive data, render the system inoperable, or even take control of the targeted device.

There are several types of malware, including those outlined in Table 2.1.

Table 2.1 Major Malware Categories

Major Malware Categories	
Viruses	A virus is a destructive string of code attached to other programs. Once the infected program is executed, the virus is installed onto the targeted machine. Viruses are spread when the infected file is transferred from one machine to the next.
Worms	A worm operates similarly to a virus in that it can be spread to a computer through an infected file. However, what sets worms apart from viruses is that they can spread without the original infected file by finding and exploiting vulnerabilities in a system or network.
Rootkits	A rootkit is a form of malware designed to grant the hacker administrative rights to a targeted computer. As rootkits are manually installed in the foundational layers of a computer's application layer, they cannot replicate in the manner that viruses do, by infected files that are shared among computers.
Spyware	Spyware refers to software that tracks a user's internet activity, gathering data such as browser history, web surfing habits, and personal information. This data is then passed along to a third party without the user's consent. Spyware is often employed by websites and applications to display targeted advertisements based on the user's web activity.
Ransomware	Ransomware is a type of malware used by cybercriminals that blocks access to a system or threatens to release sensitive information unless a sum of money is paid as ransom. Unlike most other types of cybercrime, hackers using ransomware notify victims of the attack and provide instructions for payment. The attackers usually request the ransom be paid in cryptocurrency to protect their anonymity.[*] The occurrence of ransomware attacks has grown considerably over the past few years, and ransomware is currently one of the most utilized forms of malware attack.[**]

[*] Greene, S. S. 2014. Security Program and Policies: Principles and Practices. 2nd ed. Indiana: Pearson Education, 231–232.

[**] Crowe, J. 2017. "Must-Know Ransomware Statistics 2017." https://www.alertlogic.com/blog/cybersecurity-statistics-2021/.

Going Deeper

Motivational Factors

Whether you find yourself in a Colonial Pipeline–scale predicament or a smaller one, it is particularly important to recognize the various objectives of different cybercriminals if organizations are to understand the types of threats they are likely to face and the types of countermeasures that should be implemented. There are many reasons cybercriminals engage in online criminal activity. For some, it might be the thrill of breaking the law with little chance of repercussions; for others, it could be the bragging rights that come with hacking a seemingly impenetrable system. The motives for cybercrime are often categorized as either financial gain, emotion, or political and ideological beliefs.

Financial Gain

Profit is considered the greatest motivator for cyberattacks against organizations. Cybercrime provides the opportunity to reap financial rewards with potentially little risk. Financial gain from cyberattacks generally takes three forms:

1. Profiting from selling stolen data
2. Extorting money from organizations by threatening to launch a cyberattack or leak sensitive information
3. Ransoming, where an organization's access to its data is prohibited until a ransom is paid[36]

Emotion

Money is by no means the only motivating factor. Many cybercrimes emerge purely out of an emotional response. A disgruntled employee, for example, may act out in anger by sabotaging an organization's networks. Cyberattacks executed out of anger tend to occur as a knee-jerk response to a particular situation. However, cybercrimes executed for revenge differ from those done in anger, as they tend to be carefully planned acts, rather than immediate responses. Hackers may also commit crimes to achieve a sense of pride or a sense of belonging within a group.

Political and Ideological Beliefs

Politically and ideologically motivated cybercriminals commit crimes to enforce their philosophical beliefs. These may include any range of hackers, from religious extremists to hacktivists (hacktivists are discussed in further detail later). Politically driven hackers tend to use the internet to spread their beliefs; attack the systems, networks, and data of their adversaries; or steal money in order to fund various political or militant activities. Cyberterrorism is one such type of threat, and refers to cybercrimes that target countries' critical infrastructure in order to disrupt key governmental services.

Types of Cybercriminals

Cybercriminals all rely heavily on vulnerabilities to launch successful cyberattacks. A vulnerability may be defined as a flaw in an organization's information infrastructure that makes it open to exploitation by a threat actor, or prone to harm from a given hazard. Vulnerabilities are often the result of human error or unknown faults in design, making it essential for organizations to ensure that proper procedures are put in place to identify any vulnerabilities as soon as possible.[37] An information infrastructure is regarded as vulnerable if a threat has the potential to undermine the confidentiality, integrity, or availability (together referred to as the CIA triad) of systems, networks, or data.

The following paragraphs discuss the most prevalent types of cybercriminals that pose threats to the security of an organization's information systems.

Lone Hackers

Lone hackers operate on an individual basis and are motivated by their own desires. These desires range from financial rewards to bragging rights. Many lone hackers exploit information systems solely for the intellectual challenge of circumventing a complex technical system. However, the potential impact of these hackers cannot be ignored. Although lone hackers do not focus primarily on financial gain, their ability to infiltrate an organization's IT infrastructure can still have disastrous consequences from both a public relations perspective and a liability perspective.

Hacktivists

Hacktivists use the internet as a platform for expressing their social, religious, or political views. Hacktivists are likely to cause noticeable damage to an organization by attempting to deface its web pages or harm its reputation.

Although hacktivists often lack the resources to launch large-scale attacks, they frequently avoid risk by acting as part of a collective, which increases their chances of anonymity.

The expertise of hacktivists ranges from simple, opportunistic methods of cyberattack to highly sophisticated methods that frequently spark debates about whether their actions classify them as freedom fighters or cyberterrorists.[38] Hacktivists utilize a variety of methods to achieve their objectives. The most frequently used methods are those that negatively impact an organization's public reputation. Therefore, typical methods include distributed denial-of\-service attacks to disrupt business operations and the defacing of web pages or the social media accounts of high-profile individuals.[39]

Hacktivists sometimes attempt to steal data or cause damage to an organization's critical systems, but their primary objective is to promote an ideology through a cyberattack against an organization that opposes their views. For some organizations, it might not be their own beliefs that make them the target of hacktivism, but the beliefs held by their clients or partners. It is ultimately widespread media exposure of the hack that drives attacks by hacktivists.[40] The typical targets of hacktivist activities are religious and governmental organizations, as well as corporations that hacktivists believe to oppose their ideological beliefs.

Petty Criminals

Petty criminals are financially motivated individuals or groups who opportunistically exploit vulnerabilities in individuals' and organizations' cybersecurity systems, as they often lack the resources necessary to launch sophisticated targeted attacks. When attempting to access secured systems or data, petty criminals rely on overlooked vulnerabilities to create a path of little resistance. The goal is to reap as much financial reward as possible while also avoiding as much risk as possible. If confronted with a robust cybersecurity system, these criminals are likely to move to another, less protected target.[41]

Petty criminals typically use malicious software to undermine organizations' cybersecurity, but they are also known to develop malware to sell to other hackers.

Organized Criminals

Criminal organizations have recognized the potential the internet holds for financial gain, making data theft the predominant form of cyberattack perpetrated by these cybercriminals. Unfortunately, the internet proves to be the perfect environment for organized crime. If the criminals have the resources and the expertise necessary to undermine cybersecurity systems, the internet provides easy access to targets. The internet also provides ample opportunity for criminals to mask their identities, especially in cases where the attacks are launched across national borders.[42]

It is specifically because of these factors that data theft is of increasing concern. There is great financial gain to be made from selling this type of information on black market sites. Organized criminal groups akin to the Mafia have started capitalizing on this form of cybercrime. These cybercriminal groups mirror many of the hierarchical structures found in conventional organized crime.

Cybercriminals who are backed by organized groups thus often have more resources at their disposal than cybercriminals who act autonomously. Unlike petty criminals, organized criminal groups are also more likely to target specific organizations, particularly those in the retail and financial sectors, using sophisticated methods such as advanced persistent threats or social engineering.[43]

Professional Criminals

Professional criminals can essentially be described as cybercriminals who have turned their criminal activities into something that closely resembles a conventional business. The professional cybercriminal's incentive is also financial, but the activities this type of criminal engages in extend beyond stealing directly from an organization.

Much like an ordinary business, professional criminals may provide a service, such as writing malicious software on request, that can be sold to those who do not have the expertise to develop their own means of cyberattack. This is known as "cybercrime as a service," and just as any business owner would be concerned with their brand reputation, professional criminals ensure that the service they offer differentiates them from other criminals in the underground market.[44]

Professionals tend to avoid riskier operations, opting more for low-profile, long-term scams like business fraud. Technology is usually used in order to maintain anonymity and avoid the consequences of being caught.[45]

Nation-States

Governments have discovered the potential power of well-resourced cyberattacks and are equipping themselves to wage cyberwar in ways that place both private- and public-sector organizations at risk. A high proportion of large, damaging attacks over the last decade can be attributed to nation-state actors.

Unlike cyberattacks launched by cybercriminals, cyberattacks between nation-states are designed to achieve political, economic, and military goals. State-sanctioned cyberattacks thus range from strategic intelligence-gathering campaigns to destructive attacks that have a physical impact on the targeted country's infrastructure. However, the targets of nation-states aren't limited to governmental organizations. Private corporations have also come under attack for the financial profit that can be accrued by selling sensitive data.[46]

In contrast to cybercriminals, state-sanctioned hackers are usually part of their country's military or intelligence agency. Rather than financial gain, these nation-state hackers act according to a state agenda, and have the resources necessary to undermine the cybersecurity efforts of both private and public industries. However, many nation-states also make use of hired experts (frequently referred to as cyber mercenaries) who have the skills needed to carry out cyberattacks.[47]

The nature of espionage has changed considerably, as organizations have become increasingly dependent on computers to run their everyday processes. Rather than having spies physically infiltrate and steal sensitive information, reconnaissance and intelligence gathering are conducted by computer technology and security experts in computer labs. Government support of these attacks means that in cases where attackers are exposed, they face a lower risk of criminal prosecution.[48]

Cyberattacks afford nation-states the ability to secretly target other nations without relying on the conspicuous type of military hardware that leads to aggressive retaliation (although cyberattacks may have the same result if discovered). The agility of cyberattacks also allows nation-states to choose from any range of targets, from privately owned corporations to multinational governmental organizations.

When exploring the link between nation-states and cyberattacks, there are several countries that feature prominently: China, Russia, North Korea, and Iran.

China

Since adopting a state-controlled economy decades ago, the People's Republic of China (PRC) has experienced considerable economic growth. In an attempt to keep up with the advances of its economic and political competitors, the Chinese government has launched multiple attacks to steal trade secrets and intellectual property from private and public companies in the United States and Europe. This campaign of economically motivated cyberespionage developed as a response to Chinese policymakers attempting to move the country away from manufacturing and a long-standing reliance on foreign technology. In fact, it was only in the 1990s that significant laws were implemented to begin combatting copyright violations in the PRC.[49]

China's stated goal is to become a world leader in science and technology. To achieve this goal, the Chinese government has invested greatly in technology, mathematics, and engineering at the university level, while promoting advanced research projects in nanotechnology, space exploration, and quantum research, to name a few. However, this has not stopped the Chinese government from sanctioning cyberespionage against foreign companies that employ high-end technology or advanced manufacturing techniques. Hackers have also targeted the information of companies in the financial, energy, pharmaceutical, and legal sectors.[50]

China's armed forces, the People's Liberation Army (PLA), defend China's illicit cyber activities as preparation for an "information war" against more technologically advanced adversaries. As a result, two groups from the PLA's cyber wing, Units 61398 and 61486, have targeted numerous programs developed by the U.S. Department of Defense to prepare for a potential conflict between the Chinese and United States militaries.[51] Even the Marriott hotel chain was caught up in the cyberespionage fray when PRC hackers gained access to the personal details of hundreds of millions of its customers. While many initially blamed criminals seeking financial gain, it later emerged that China's espionage efforts were the source.[52]

China's cyber activities also include attacks against organizations that promote information that conflicts with the Chinese government's policies. The PRC's "Great Firewall" combines numerous policies and technologies to regulate the Chinese population's access to foreign websites, and heavily censor information-sharing through the internet. The aim is not just to censor information from external sources but also to nurture China's domestic companies by forcing foreign internet companies to adhere to domestic regulations that limit their ability to deliver products.

Russia
Much like China, Russia has special military units whose sole purpose is to wage cyberwar. However, it is far more difficult to connect cyberattacks that originate from Russia with the Russian

government. Cyberattacks from Russia are frequently traced back to organized cybercriminals or hacktivist groups. However, the high-profile targets that have fallen victim to Russian hackers (such as Ukraine's power grid, for example) have led to the conclusion that these civilian hackers are supported by the Russian government.

Russia's cyber activities may be further motivated by the perception that in the near future, a country's superiority will be dictated by its capability to wage a war of information. In this "information war," a country's superiority is dictated not by military hardware alone, but also by campaigns of informational deception.

Much of Russia's new approach to power emerged as a result of pro-Kremlin leaders being replaced by democratically elected governments friendly with the West throughout Eastern Europe and Central Asia. Russia considered these revolutions to be part of U.S.-backed operations meant to compromise its allies and the Russian state. Key Russian military planners thus concluded that to counter a perceived threat from the United States, similar cyber operations needed to be executed to enforce Russia's sovereignty.[53]

Most cybercrimes that originate in Russia are aimed at the networks of financial institutions in the West. This is because cybercrimes against targets outside of Russia are less likely to be investigated by law-enforcement agencies. These cybercrimes are also frequently backed by Russian organized crime groups, who have the resources necessary to conduct sophisticated, well-financed cyber operations.

North Korea

Following North Korea's split from South Korea after World War II, Kim Il-sung and Kim Jong-il, North Korea's first two "supreme leaders," established a large conventional military to match that of its most direct adversaries, South Korea and the United States. However, North Korea does not have the resources necessary to face the United States and South Korea in a prolonged conventional military engagement, and therefore relies on an asymmetric military strategy to disrupt its rivals. An asymmetric strategy is one that attacks an adversary's vulnerabilities, rather than risking a head-on confrontation.[54]

Kim Jong-un, North Korea's current leader, has therefore expanded the country's military to include a specialized cyber unit known as Bureau 121, whose purpose is to wage an unconventional cyberwar against South Korea and the United States. Aligning with its asymmetric strategy, North Korea's cyber activities attempt to disrupt conventional operations during a confrontation, and execute disruptive provocations during times of peace that offset their adversaries' technological advantage. As a result, the sophistication and frequency of North Korean cyberattacks have risen sharply over the last decade.

North Korea's cyber operations are motivated by a number of factors, including espionage, monetary gain, intimidation, and retaliation.[55]

Over the past several years, North Korean cyber operatives have focused their cyber activities on financially motivated attacks. Since 2016, North Korean hackers have unleashed an unprecedented wave of ransomware attacks for extortion, hacks of automatic teller machines in developing countries, and theft of funds from financial institutions like the central bank of Bangladesh and cryptocurrency exchanges. In early 2020, the U.S. Department of Homeland Security issued a high-profile report asserting that North Korea's "malicious cyber activities threaten the United States and the broader international community and, in particular, pose a significant threat to the integrity and stability of the international financial system."[56]

Iran

Iran's current cyber capabilities can be traced to two pivotal turning points. The first is the Green Revolution, which occurred in 2009. During the Green Revolution, the Iranian regime faced anti-regime protests that were largely arranged through social media. As a result, the regime imposed harsh internet censorship, especially in the use of social media websites, and intensified cyber surveillance. The Iranian Cyber Army also launched numerous attacks against websites that belonged to groups supporting the anti-regime protests.[57]

The second incident was a series of attacks that targeted Iran's aspiring nuclear program. In 2010, Iran's nuclear facility in Natanz was disrupted when a string of malicious code caused critical failures in the equipment necessary to produce enriched uranium. Iran's nuclear production slowed down significantly during the time that the virus was active. Following this, two additional advanced types of malware were found on Iran's computer networks, one in September 2011 and another in May 2012, which targeted the Ministry of Petroleum's websites.[58]

In response to these attacks, the Supreme Leader of the Islamic Republic, Ali Khamenei, established the Supreme Council of Cyberspace to act as a centralized entity that deals with all decision-making that relates to cyber activities. Iran's cyber operations are now considered a fundamental aspect of the regime's national security strategy, and have developed from simple acts of retaliation against activist groups to sophisticated attacks with the potential to disrupt critical infrastructure.

Taking Action

An important first step for organizations is to build awareness of the common cyber threats facing your specific industry. Each sector has its own cyber risk profile. That is, each sector will have different circumstances that lead to different combinations of threat actors, motives, types of attack, and malware. Awareness of the configuration dominant within your own sector will help you better defend your organization. While far from comprehensive, the sector risk profiles that follow provide a useful guide for organizations to begin thinking about how and why they may be targeted based on their organizational context. Beyond understanding sectoral risks, it is important to engage with other organizations in your sector to access active threat intelligence.

Understanding the Threats to Your Sector

Finance

The financial sector is incredibly diverse, with a myriad of subsectors—such as the insurance and investment industries and credit organizations—that constitute the wider global economy. Many financial services providers depend on other financial services providers for their own operation. As such, the fintech that enables these financial services plays an instrumental role in ensuring their continued operation. Of particular importance in the finance industry is the ability to conduct transactions without fault, thereby creating public trust and support for the systems on which financial organizations depend.[59] Doubt could be cast on public trust in the financial system when banks are targeted by hackers that manage to gain access to networks that contain sensitive data, such as customers' savings and checking account information. Such cyberattacks make banks vulnerable to business operational risk and reputational risk. It is thus vital for financial institutions to ensure the confidentiality and integrity of their financial data, and secure the networks that process it.

Healthcare

Information is crucial to the healthcare sector, as almost all healthcare-related services depend on sensitive data being transferred between devices on a large-scale network. It is this sensitive data that makes the healthcare sector one of the fastest-growing targets of cyberattacks over recent years, as patient data is frequently stolen or held for ransom.[60]

The prevalence of cyberattacks against the healthcare industry is increasing in large part due to the exposure of the industry to threats in the cyber landscape through the inherent technical vulnerabilities of OT devices connected online. The healthcare industry is growing increasingly dependent on digital infrastructure to manage their IoT-enabled medical devices, patient records, and online consumer applications. This has the added effect of increasing the potential entry points for cybercriminals to strike.[61]

Manufacturing

Companies in the manufacturing industry are making great strides in the digital transformation of their business operations. Global networks are becoming increasingly popular as companies grow their areas of influence, and advanced manufacturing technologies are continuously being implemented to keep up with the need for producing current products.[62] However, as is the case with other sectors discussed here, when organizations increase their cyber footprint, they expand their chances of being targeted in cyberattacks.

A dominant concept in advanced manufacturing technology is Industry 4.0, which refers to the current trend in manufacturing to make use of cyber-physical systems (OT) and large-scale interconnectedness between internal and external productive units. Cybercriminals have been able to capitalize on this industrial-scale connectivity between systems and manufacturing units by exploiting vulnerabilities found in unsecured supply chains, service providers, and partners.[63]

Past cyberattacks on the manufacturing industry have shown a high prevalence of malware attacks aimed at stealing sensitive data and intellectual property from both large and small companies.[64] However, cyberattacks launched against manufacturers have also resulted in physical damage to manufacturing equipment.

Education

The current nature of educational institutions makes them especially prone to cyberattacks aimed at stealing data in the form of user credentials and other personal information. Many universities foster a culture of open networks and information-sharing. Although this increases both student and public access to valuable knowledge, the ease of access to networks used by educational institutions also places them at considerable risk of threat.[65]

In higher education, for example, data is frequently shared across departments and stored on various systems throughout the institution. The types of data stored on these systems include financial information (relating to student tuition, for example), information relating to the university's operations, and, in many cases, medical information. The type of attack launched against universities depends largely on the size of the university, with high-profile, research-based universities being at particular risk of attacks from nation-states, organized crime, and hacktivists. Smaller-scale universities are far from immune, and frequently suffer from stolen or compromised data.[66]

Power and Utilities

The power and utilities sectors are undergoing a tremendous shift in the use of information technology and operational technology to improve operational processes. However, as cyberattacks become more sophisticated, fears arise about the impact this might have on the safety of critical infrastructure.

The energy business relies on an electricity grid to distribute power generated by the power plant to electricity users. This process relies on a number of different components functioning at optimal capacity. All necessary components, such as generating stations, transformers, and distribution lines (to name a few), are connected to a centralized power grid.[67]

Together, all the elements that constitute the power grid are controlled by operational technology called industrial control systems (ICS), which operate in a loop to continually check that each component in the power grid is functioning as it should. Supervisory control and data acquisition (SCADA) systems, which utilize remote terminals to control the switches that regulate electricity production, have also undergone significant changes. SCADA systems have migrated online, making them easier to access from a variety of devices.[68]

The power and utilities sectors are uniquely positioned, as cyberattacks not only pose a risk to business operations, but also create a national security issue. The U.S. economy, for example, is massively dependent on the effective distribution of electricity for keeping key industries functional. In light of this, there has been an increase in investments in impressive information security systems that regulate access to industrial control and SCADA systems.

Retail

As with the other sectors discussed in this chapter, the retail sector is undergoing a number of changes to keep up with the changing nature of doing business in an increasingly online world. A key driving force in this regard is responding to the needs of consumers, who expect mobility in their shopping experiences, pushing more retailers to migrate their services onto online platforms. Retailers have always been a popular target for crime, but the growing dependence on integrating information systems has exposed them to a new front in their struggle with criminals.

Considering that a single point-of-sale (POS) system may process thousands of transactions every day, cybercriminals have been quick to design malware with the capacity to breach retailers' cybersecurity and capture credit card data when payments are made. Many retailers still employ older, outdated operating systems. Outdated operating systems create dangerous vulnerabilities in cybersecurity because they are not updated to deal with newer forms of malware. In some cases, once hackers can access a POS system, it becomes relatively easy for them to identify and collect the necessary data, as the credit and debit card credentials are presented in clear text due to a lack of encryption. Although more secure systems have been developed, many retailers have been slow to embrace more secure technologies and cybersecurity strategies that could improve the safety of sensitive data.[69]

Sectoral Threat Intelligence

While it is useful to know which systems, networks, and data may be attractive to attackers for each sector, it is equally important to be continuously updated about active threats to the sector. One means for accessing this information is to join an Information Sharing and Analysis Center (ISAC) for your sector. ISACs are privately run but generally have direct ties to a government sponsor and are responsible for aggregating and providing access to best practices for the sector and sharing actionable threat intelligence. For example, in the wake of the DarkSide ransomware attack, the Oil and Natural Gas ISAC likely disseminated alerts to its members to be on the lookout for malicious activity in the case that DarkSide was specifically targeting pipelines. Such alerts are useful because organizations within a sector often make use of similar digital assets that may be purpose-built for their industry. An attack on one organization's assets (perhaps a programmable logic controller control system) can equally be applied to similar assets in other organizations.

Unfortunately, not all ISACS are created equal. Some have members that actively contribute to threat information sharing, whereas others exclusively rely on intelligence from government sponsors. One ISAC that has a particularly good reputation for actively sharing information among its members is the Financial Services ISAC. Perhaps one reason for their success is that participation is incentivized and even mandated by industry standards and through regulatory requirements. The Financial Services ISAC is among the most established, whereas other industries are just getting started but eager to make progress—such as the much-anticipated and much-needed Space ISAC. Your organization should check to see if it is a member of its respective sector's ISAC and if not, inquire about joining. It could become an essential tool in your Embedded Endurance quiver.

Action on the Front Lines

Successfully predicting a ransomware attack on a specific Friday is nearly impossible. Fortunately, leading Embedded Endurance efforts in your organization does not require omniscience. CEO Joseph Blount should have anticipated the range of attackers who might target Colonial Pipeline due to the company's importance. This critical review, in turn, could have undergirded the technical, procedural, and organizational changes that might have kept Colonial Pipeline out of the headlines, or at least reduced the damage it suffered.

This component of the Embedded Endurance strategy is grounded in field-tested experience. While spending time at NASA's Jet Propulsion Laboratory (JPL), Falco worked with cybersecurity researchers, data scientists, and mission risk managers. An unofficial stance long taken by NASA was that because their efforts were entirely peaceful, collaborative, open, and focused on scientific exploration, cybersecurity was not high on their priority list. The thought was: "Why would someone want to harm us?" However, the relatively small but highly advanced team focusing on cybersecurity of mission systems at the space juggernaut had a strong hypothesis. NASA JPL and its contractors are at the bleeding edge of technological development, which results in the constant generation of innovative intellectual property (IP). Such IP is useful not only for creating spacecrafts, but also for developing other industrial and military technology. Over years of incidents, it has become clearer that nation-states are engaging in industrial espionage and targeting NASA JPL's systems for the betterment of their own space programs and economic development.[70] With this insight, NASA JPL has enacted specific measures to safeguard their IP against this threat. Threat actors' motivations are highly variable, requiring an Embedded Endurance strategy to address them accordingly.

Main Takeaway

Know your enemy. While cyberattacks are carried out through digital means, remember that there are people on the other side of the keyboard. Attackers have their own motives and goals, and use attacks that are often specific to your organization. Understanding who has the motive to attack your organization, anticipating their attack type, and being aware of potential malware mechanisms that can be used against your organization are all part of a delicate, ongoing negotiation-type process with cyber adversaries and are key to establishing your organization's Embedded Endurance. Each sector will have specific circumstances that make it attractive to specific attackers and different attack types; risk management measures need to be taken based on these unique circumstances.

3

How Do I Assess Our Cyber Risk?

*Identifying and characterizing the cyber risk unique to your
critical systems, networks, and data*

Case Study

The Attack

On December 23, 2015, the world's first cyberattack to disrupt energy companies at scale struck Ukraine's power grid,[1] knocking
out electricity for 225,000 citizens.[2] Three energy companies
suffered damage almost simultaneously in the well-coordinated
strike.[3] Workers watched helplessly in real time as hackers remotely
commandeered their cursors and wreaked havoc.[4]

The attackers targeted the utilities' substations, which are scattered
across power grids and perform crucial distribution and conversion
roles. By opening circuit breakers in at least fifty-seven substations,[5]
the strike blanketed more than 100 communities with complete
blackouts and hit almost 200 more with partial blackouts.[6]

How It Happened

The hackers knew closing the breakers could make for a quick fix,
so they had bolstered their attack to prevent this. They shut down
a main data center and two control centers, blinding workers to the
chaos.[7] At one company they hit an internal telephone server, thus

Confronting Cyber Risk. Gregory Falco and Eric Rosenbach, Oxford University Press. © Oxford University Press
2022. DOI: 10.1093/oso/9780197526545.003.0003

blocking communications with other offices and substations.[8] Bogus phone calls flooded call centers while real customers struggled to get through, choking information flows between the companies and the public.[9]

Finally, the attack wiped files from a host of devices—rendering affected IT systems at all three companies brain-dead—and corrupted critical equipment at the substations.[10] This last move severed communications between control centers and the impacted field devices; even if operators identified the problem, they still could not close the breakers remotely.[11]

Restoring Power

Although companies could not restore power by remotely resetting breakers,[12] Soviet-era manual controls allowed crews to restore power within six hours.[13] Later, the companies discovered the corrupted substation equipment was irreparable, forcing them to depend on these manual controls for months.[14]

Such a solution would likely be impossible in the United States. Many control systems in our own power grid do not have manual backups.[15] Even for utilities that have the capability, do they have the know-how? The Ukrainian companies failed to have a plan prepared for this incident, so it was their teams' experience with "manual mode" that enabled their quick recovery.[16]

Broader factors also mitigated the disruption. Due to a recent history of unreliable electricity, it is standard practice for Ukrainian critical services to keep backup generators. And weather the day of the outage was significantly warmer than usual, sparing residents from the standard December freeze.[17]

How to Do Better

Still, the energy companies themselves are far from blameless. As one researcher at the cybersecurity firm ESET concluded, "It shouldn't have been so easy for the attackers."[18] Among other issues, tight connections between business and control IT systems gave hackers wide access across networks, control over remote access was loose,[19] and—while monitoring industrial control systems is often relatively easy—the companies' detection methods were subpar.[20]

The lesson here is not to use outdated systems. The lucky escape they provided Ukraine in this case is the exception to the rule; cyber history is replete with examples of outmoded equipment and software sabotaging cyber risk management efforts.

In fact, while the world heard much about the energy companies discussed here, these were not the only organizations attacked that day. At least three other companies from critical infrastructure sectors were targeted in the same campaign, but managed to dodge operational impacts.[21] Due to security concerns, information on these organizations' defenses is scarce (Ukraine is not eager to aid attackers by spilling details). However, we do know that one of these success stories involved implementing recommended practices for monitoring industrial control systems networks.[22]

The real takeaway is the importance of identifying critical systems, networks, and data before adversaries do. As the attackers in this case study demonstrated, hackers will think and work hard to design an attack that targets your organization's greatest weaknesses and takes advantage of flaws in your response plans. The best way to stay a few steps ahead of them is to implement this thought process yourself. Doing so allows you to better characterize the vulnerabilities in your organization, more fully assess the potential business impact of a cyberattack, and thus answer the question "How do I assess our cyber risk?"

Why It Matters

No good doctor would prescribe a cure before trying to properly diagnose a patient's condition. No good general makes reforms without first understanding the weaknesses of the command in question. Similarly, a risk assessment is a prerequisite for mitigating your organization's cyber risk.

An objective for any organization is to protect the confidentiality, integrity, and availability (known as the CIA triad) of critical assets. Critical assets can be described as prioritized systems, networks, and data that enable the organization to function. Given the complexities of an organization's technology architecture and dataflows, it is not as easy as it sounds. However, in this chapter we will discuss steps that leaders of any organization can take to make sense of the cyber risks facing them, and to profile those risks' potential for impacting their bottom line.

Key Concepts

1. Characterizing cyber risk
2. Identifying critical assets

Characterizing Cyber Risk

Any organization's Embedded Endurance strategy should aim to protect the confidentiality, integrity, and availability of its information assets. Altogether, these three elements are referred to as the CIA triad and characterize the type of cyber risk to any given system, network, or data. It is crucial that when cybersecurity strategies are developed, the consequent policies and procedures are aligned with business objectives in such a way that they support the CIA triad of an organization's information systems. This support should extend to all information assets, whether managed by the organization or handled by third-party services.

Confidentiality
Confidentiality refers to the need to keep sensitive information private. Information carries great value in the digital world, and organizations need to ensure that sensitive data is restricted to appropriate individuals.

Hackers attempt to steal sensitive information for various reasons, including making money, stealing intellectual property, and collecting intelligence. The vast majority of hackers steal information to make money. For example, hackers working as part of an organized criminal group would steal any information that would help them steal funds, such as transaction histories, bank account information, and customer credit card credentials. The Chinese intelligence services, however, are well known for stealing valuable intellectual property and sensitive information about pending energy transactions. Other intelligence agencies, like the Russian Federal Security Service, conduct hacks to collect intelligence information. The fact that most cyberattacks occur because nefarious actors want to steal data makes preventative measures all the more vital.

Integrity

Integrity refers to the consistency of systems, networks, and data. The integrity of a system or data is maintained by preventing unauthorized or unintentional alterations, and ensuring that the system or data appears as intended when accessed by a user. Maintaining integrity includes preemption and resilience measures that both restrict users' editing rights and make it possible to recover from any unapproved changes.[23]

Cyberattacks that affect the integrity of an organization's information systems are likely to increase as methods of attack become increasingly sophisticated. Organizations may suffer several effects of these attacks, such as reputational damage in instances when the public no longer trusts the information they receive from an organization. The financial industry is especially sensitive to this form of attack, as corporations rely heavily on accurate financial reporting and transaction registers used for contractual, compliance, and reporting obligations.

Availability

An information asset is considered available if authorized users can freely access its systems, networks, or data. In order to achieve availability of information assets, network and system administrators need to ensure that a fully operational system environment is maintained at all times.

In terms of maintaining the availability of information systems in the face of potential cyberattacks, organizations need to be wary of the types of cyberattacks that impede users' access to critical assets. Ransomware and distributed denial-of-service attacks are both examples where hacks may lead to the total loss of the availability of information systems. Organizations thus cannot rely on preventative measures alone to mitigate the threat of attack, but must also implement incident response plans that allow them to recover access to information systems in a timely manner when attacks do occur.[24]

Think about the assets your organization depends on for its daily operations. Given the shift toward remote work that the COVID-19 pandemic accelerated, it is important to consider how assets may or may not extend beyond your organization's physical space. What would happen if the confidentiality, integrity, or availability of those systems become compromised? Not only does the Ukraine case underscore the dangers facing a single organization, but it also reminds us that all modern organizations are reliant upon other enterprises and networks and thus susceptible to ripple effects from attacks on them.

Identifying Critical Assets

Systems, networks, and data are fundamental to any digital organization, but not all digital assets are of equal importance. In what follows we describe how to categorize different assets, which will help you begin to assess their criticality to your organization.

Critical Systems
Organizations depend on various systems to meet their operational goals. The importance of specific systems varies by organization, and the failure of a digital system could have different operational

consequences depending on its importance to an organization. In some cases, the failure of a system results in heavy economic loss or even physical harm to assets or personnel. These critical systems can be divided into three categories:

1. **Mission-critical systems:** These are the systems that are responsible for executing the functions organizations depend on to meet their stated goals. Failure of mission-critical systems may result in an organization's complete inability to continue its key operations.

2. **Business-critical systems:** These systems have a specific function in the effective delivery of an organization's service but are not responsible for the overall operation of the organization. Unlike mission-critical systems, the failure of a business-critical system does not result in a complete shutdown of an organization's services. Instead, the failure of business-critical systems impairs or interrupts the organization's service for some length of time, resulting in considerable economic loss. Business-critical systems focus on the management of assets. While the systems themselves might not shut down, the ability to manage them could be hindered. Mission-focused systems can continue their operations, but the business-critical systems managing them can be taken offline.

3. **Safety-critical systems:** These are the systems that protect the physical safety of an organization's personnel and the environment. Failures in safety-critical systems have the potential for causing damage to the environment or placing human life at risk.

Critical Networks

Networks play an instrumental role in supporting critical business functions by ensuring accessibility to important data. Depending on their industry, product, and range of information assets, an organization may have networks of varying complexity. Most organizations use more than one type of network to maintain their public online presence, internal operations, access to information assets, data backups, and client- or customer-facing operations.[25]

Each type of network comprises a piece of the overall IT infrastructure. Just as each type of network contributes a specific capability to the organization, each network is susceptible to specific attacks and vulnerabilities.

Networks that transmit data in and out of the organization are often the most logical point of attack. Given that most organizations use more than one distinct type of network, executive decision-making regarding cybersecurity is often compromised by a lack of visibility into the performance and security of the organization's networks.[26] Managers must have a clear understanding of the various facets of modern networked systems and the unique risks they pose.

From a technical perspective, you do not need to know the ins and outs of installing or securing these networks, but basic knowledge of the function of each type of network in a typical business is essential to understanding how each network functions as an asset, and what compromising each network may mean for risk. The network types include:

- **Business and administration networks:** Engaged for the management of key business processes, decision-making, and business resources to achieve an organization's mission
- **Operational and service delivery networks:** Engaged for the control of specific processes such as commanding a remote asset to perform a unique function in order to deliver a service to end users
- **Communication networks:** Engaged for creating an intranet or private network that centralizes business information such as important news, events, policies, operations instructions, or employee contact details.

Critical Data

The third asset critical to an organization's information systems is its data. There are seven major categories of data that organizations should prioritize when developing an Embedded Endurance risk mitigation strategy. Categories of critical data include, but are not limited to, personally identifiable information (PII), financial data, health data or protected health information (PHI), education data, payment card data, credentials, and intellectual property. These types of data represent business operational, reputational, and litigation risks if either their confidentiality or integrity is compromised.

Threat actors weigh the risks of attempting a data breach with the potential return on investment (ROI) to be gained from accessing specific data. The data that has high ROI varies between sectors; the seven general data categories are useful starting points for thinking about data risk to your organization. Some of these categories relate more specifically to particular industries, while others can relate to any sector.

Indeed, in the era of widespread artificial intelligence technologies, many companies find that data is more important than ever to their core decision-making and operational processes. Even the best machine learning models are only as good as the pool of data upon which they rely to recognize patterns, make decisions, and provide value. The integrity and availability components of the CIA triad are especially important given these ongoing AI trends. Capturing value from wider swaths of data requires integrity in your organization's long-term data management techniques. As the standard for what constitutes "big data" continues to climb, ensuring on-demand availability of that information requires more foresight and effort. Unfortunately, the growing data troves entice hackers with higher-value targets, and even data that resists exfiltration can become collateral damage if it is corrupted during an attack.

Going Deeper

Identifying Business Impact

Business impact analysis is a process that assesses the potential impact of an interruption to business operations that results from an emergency or accident.[27] In this case, BIA will be utilized to identify critical elements of an organization's digital assets based on the consequences of being compromised. In order to do so, BIA correlates systems, networks, and data with the organization's stated mission, and identifies the most critical assets based on the cost that the disruption would incur.

There are three steps involved in completing a BIA:[28]

1. **Determine mission/business processes and recovery criticality:** The first step involves identifying the business processes that are supported by the system under consideration, and evaluating the impact in the event that the system is disrupted. The organization should also assess the maximum time that it can afford for a system to be offline while still being able to meet its mission.

2. **Identify resource requirements:** The assessor should also identify the resources necessary to resume business operations as soon as possible. Resources may include software, personnel, hardware, and critical system components.

3. **Identify recovery priorities for system resources:** Based on the information collected during the first two steps, the assessor links systems to the business mission and important processes. In doing so, systems can be arranged according to priority levels for implementing recovery activities.

Conducting a BIA has three major benefits. First, through this process your organization will improve its defenses. The hackers in the case study presented at the start of this chapter had done their homework. They had studied Ukraine's power grid not only to understand the system's vulnerabilities, but also to anticipate weaknesses in the network operators' response. Completing the three steps just described will help you build defenses and response protocols that outsmart would-be attackers.

Second, it will improve your organization's reaction speed in the event of an attack. The aftermath of a cyberattack is chaotic. Organizational confusion about the relative importance of various business processes only adds to the turbulence. Having identified your organization's most critical functions beforehand will allow you to more effectively define objectives and make the most efficient use of limited resources to achieve them.

Finally, a BIA will help you quantify the total cost of a cyberattack. Not only is this important for communicating with external stakeholders such as investors and the media, but it is also essential for maximizing your organization's potential for recuperating losses through insurance. The landscape of cyberattack insurance is shifting and will continue to do so. However, a constant amid the churn is that a clear, quantifiable articulation of the total damage due to an attack (or even an accident) is a critical element of any successful insurance claim.

The Evolving Digital Landscape

Given the constantly changing landscape of technology advancements, the critical systems, networks, and data that your organization engages could be considerably different over time. For example, in the early 2000s most organizations maintained their own, on-premise server infrastructure, with much of this equipment tucked away in a closet—something that only the "IT people" knew about. These server racks would have certainly been considered critical systems. Today though, many companies use virtualized cloud server infrastructure to host and run digital operations that are maintained by a third-party provider. Given the security sophistication of major cloud service providers such as Amazon Web Services (AWS) or Microsoft Azure, your organization can be less concerned with these systems' security directly; should an attacker target your organization, they are highly likely to seek a different attack surface rather than first hacking into AWS.

The racks in the closet are now interesting relics or sometimes serve as backups in the case of a major cloud failure (which would have consequences impacting many far beyond your organization). While they would have originally been considered critical systems, your cloud provider is now the critical system. In terms of your BIA when engaging cloud services, you will want to focus on securely configuring your integration with virtualized systems, rather than having to worry about the racks themselves.

The evolving technology landscape not only can impact existing systems, networks, and data that have received upgrades. It also applies to new technology that your organization may not have even considered using—let alone rely on—in the past.

An example of such technology is Internet of Things devices. Building managers and operators historically needed to send an operator to each building they managed and walk around tuning thermostats and turning lights on and off in order to save energy and costs. With the advent of "smart buildings" where thermostats and lights are connected to the internet and controlled via a centralized platform, there can be considerable cost savings and operational efficiency. Previously building operators may not have thought about the cybersecurity of lights and heating, ventilation, and air-conditioning (HVAC), but now that lights and HVAC are IoT devices, they certainly will be considered critical systems in the context of security.

Another major change to the digital landscape is the abundance of publicly available, personal data on your employees and your business. With the growth of social media, online advertising, and mobile device usage, the technology landscape increasingly is capturing more personal information about users. Hackers can use this personal information—for example, an employee's frequently visited locations or hobbies—to build trust with employees and gain access to their company login credentials or knowledge of the business's operations. This technique is called social engineering. Hackers might also use information from social media to craft a more effective phishing attack. For example, imagine that an employee posts a picture on social media of the team outing to a particular bowling alley; a hacker sees this picture and uses LinkedIn to find a procurement associate at the same company. The hacker, pretending to be the bowling alley, then sends a "Late Invoice—Urgent Payment" email to the procurement associate, specifying the date of the service provided and the name of an employee contact on the team (all captured from social media). The procurement associate does a cursory check with the employee, who confirms they did indeed have an event at the bowling alley, and clicks on the link for payment the hacker has sent. The link could contain malware, a route for fraudulent payment, or any number of attacks. Even online advertising profiles of users, which advertising companies claim are anonymized, can be de-anonymized, revealing valuable personal information about your employees, such as their internet searches, their social security number (SSN), their medical records, and more—all of which can be exploited to manipulate your employees and gain access to your business.

The artificial intelligence revolution is another example of technological evolution that requires due care concerning security. AI algorithms power a number of systems with which we interact every day, from the recommendation engines informing what we read and watch to the computers generating weather forecasts. Many of AI's cybersecurity issues overlap with those present in IoT devices, particularly as AI-controlled autonomous systems proliferate. Still, AI systems' heavy reliance on data presents new attack pathways for hackers seeking to disrupt them, as do "adversarial" attacks that exploit weaknesses in the algorithms themselves. There's also the potential for attackers to leverage their own AI systems—for example, to aid in the search for weaknesses in a target's defense. Finally, many of the more traditional cyberattacks can be just as effective against AI systems—after all, the humans who work on machine learning systems are just as susceptible to phishing attacks as the rest of us. As the influence of AI technologies in our lives grows, so too does the magnitude of the cybersecurity risks they bring.

The increasingly distributed nature of systems, networks, and data also adds to the complexity of identifying what is critical. The advent of distributed ledgers (e.g., blockchain technology) has improved awareness of distributed computing, where a computing task may be broken up and performed across multiple systems. There are many security benefits to using distributed systems, but challenges exist too. For example, instead of having to worry about the security of a single, centralized system, you now need to be concerned about many interconnected and distributed systems—some of which are not always under your control. An example may be engaging satellite communications infrastructure owned by third parties but critical to your own communication networks. Doing so provides unprecedented capability and flexibility, but also extends your attack surface. For example, now you are vulnerable not only to phishing attacks directed at your own employees, but also to those directed at the employees of the satellite communications infrastructure provider. Considering how you engage with such assets when you have no physical access to them and limited control is crucial to determining how to enact an Embedded Endurance strategy.

Sometimes your critical systems, networks, and data will change for reasons beyond technology advancement. The COVID-19 pandemic drove an immense shift toward remote work almost overnight. For the myriad organizations that have adopted these work-from-home arrangements on a more permanent basis, it is important to begin classifying the remote-enabling systems, networks, and data as critical and prioritizing them accordingly in the process of conducting risk assessments. Having more employees working from home increases the amount of your organization's data that flows over a broader range of networks. Not only does this open avenues of attack for hackers, but it can also limit your organizational resilience in the wake of an attack. Among other obstacles, it may obfuscate your attempts to assess the full extent of the damage, communicate with key players, or adopt stopgap solutions.

The evolving digital landscape—be it a function of technology advancement or because of other organizational culture and process shifts—presents the need for a continuous reassessment of critical systems, networks, and data. This is not a one-time analysis, but something that should be completed on an annual basis at least.

Taking Action

There's no one-size-fits-all method for assessing cyber risk. Our proposed approach of identifying critical systems, networks, and data and then characterizing their risk is one approach that is relatively straightforward and does not require considerable resources to accomplish. Here are some concrete actions that can be taken toward starting this assessment.

Identify Your Systems, Networks, and Data

Many organizations do not have an inventory of their systems, networks, and data. The first step to determining what is deemed critical is to take stock of what exists. Only after you are aware of what types of systems, networks, and data your organization holds can you begin to determine which are mission-, business-, and safety-critical, as defined previously. Conducting an asset inventory is a tedious undertaking but essential should you seek to assess your cyber risk.

Characterize the Threats to Your Systems, Networks, and Data

Each asset you have determined to be critical will have a different risk profile. This is the case not only at an organization-by-organization level but even within a single organization, because each asset has its own unique purpose and is engaged differently by disparate stakeholders. For each critical asset, it is important to assess if the worst-case scenario is characterized as a confidentiality breach, integrity degradation, or availability disruption. Often, a cyberattack will result in all three; however, depending on the system and organizational context, the focus of the attack will likely be on one of the three issues. For example, an attack against an electric utility that operates a wide variety of control systems and associated operational technologies may lose data confidentiality, integrity, and availability; however, given the service-level agreements that a utility has with regulators and its customers, the most critical threat is a compromise of availability. By applying this systematic approach to your own critical systems, networks, and data and documenting which threats become the most relevant for each asset, you will have a stronger handle on the magnitude of the specific incident when your organization is inevitably attacked.

Action on the Front Lines

The Ukrainian grid case study is interesting because of the clear Embedded Endurance dichotomy: three targeted energy companies fell victim to the attacks, while at least three others did not. Those that suffered could have made better use of cyber risk assessment and monitoring tools, and would be smart to look to their more successful neighbors for ideas. In this way one organization's Embedded Endurance strategy can even extend beyond its own perimeter to improve outcomes across entire regions and sectors.

In the wake of the world's most destructive cyberattack, conducted by Iranian cyber operators against Saudi Aramco, deputy assistant secretary of defense Eric Rosenbach was deployed by the secretary of defense to Saudi Arabia. The attack destroyed 35,000 computers in a few hours and rendered the world's largest energy producer nearly useless. Rosenbach's job was to work with the deputy minister of defense, Mohammad bin-Salman,[29] to bolster Saudi Arabia's cyber defenses against future attacks on critical infrastructure. The Iranian attack, which targeted Saudi Aramco's administrative business networks, did not impact the critical SCADA networks that supported Aramco's energy production and transport infrastructure. Destruction of these SCADA networks would have resulted in a months-long disruption of production and delivery capacity, which would have significantly impacted world energy supplies and markets. The terrifying reality, however, is that the Iranian cyber operators could have destroyed the SCADA networks because they were directly connected to the same targeted business networks. The reason Aramco escaped the full impact of an attack was . . . luck.

The primary lesson for Rosenbach was that Aramco, and Saudi Arabia in general at the time, lacked any basic risk mitigation strategy that involved identifying and protecting critical networks, systems, or data. That failure of leadership to enact a strategy nearly destabilized world energy markets and, potentially, could have resulted in armed conflict in the Gulf region.

Main Takeaway

Assessing cyber risk is about more than creating a laundry list of the vulnerabilities of your technology or quantifying the likelihood of a major loss event. It is about conducting a business impact analysis in relation to your critical systems, networks, and data so that you can successfully rank—and respond to—future incidents accordingly. As you can see, the Embedded Endurance perspective for assessing cyber risk is essential. Identifying which of your organization's systems, networks, and data are truly critical is impossible without understanding both how they relate to each other and how they serve your business priorities.

4

What Do I Need to Know About Cyber Frameworks, Standards, and Laws?

Distilling the complex landscape of cyber risk laws, requirements, and standards

Case Study

As the European Union's General Data Protection Regulation (GDPR) neared implementation, all corners of the data world asked whether the wide-ranging regulation would be more fizzle or bang. In some ways the atmosphere resembled that preceding Y2K nearly two decades prior. But unlike the Y2K hype, GDPR's impact following its May 25, 2018, entry into force vindicated the commotion preceding it.

What Happened?

Dwight Barns, CEO of Nielsen Holdings PLC, assured the public that GDPR's impact on his firm would be a fizzle.[1] His company— a market research firm with an emphasis on media ratings and e-commerce[2]—relied on large sets of consumer data from providers like Facebook. The possibility that GDPR could upend Nielsen's

Confronting Cyber Risk. Gregory Falco and Eric Rosenbach, Oxford University Press. © Oxford University Press 2022. DOI: 10.1093/oso/9780197526545.003.0004

access to the data underlying much of its valuable analysis concerned investors.[3]

On an April conference call, Barns reassured his audience. He promised, "We're ready for this," and projected that "we see the greater focus on privacy, including GDPR, as a net positive for our position in the marketplace."[4] Even days after GDPR's implementation, Barns boasted at a conference that "we still have the access to all the data that we need for our measurement products" and that GDPR had "been more of a non-event from our side as compared to how it played out for some others."[5]

But while Barns promised a fizzle, the truth was that GDPR hit Nielsen with a bang. Despite statements as late as June that the company was on track to hit its financial targets,[6] the company in July issued second-quarter results and updated forecasts that contradicted previous predictions.[7] This included a $250 million reduction in its free cash flow forecast for 2018—a cut that slashed the annual estimate itself by nearly a third.[8] Similarly grim were the revisions to the company's projected net income and EBITDA margin growth.[9]

Company officials explicitly cited GDPR as a cause of this revision. CFO Jamere Jackson admitted, "We are seeing some short-term pressure from GDPR and privacy changes that are impacting our second quarter results and 2018 outlook."[10] He later explained, "Our results were significantly below our expectations as revenues were impacted by GDPR and changes to the consumer data privacy landscape."[11]

The Impact

These jarring announcements pushed Nielsen's stock into a nosedive, dropping its value by 25 percent.[12] The debacle also cost Barns his job: when Nielsen published the new numbers it also announced Barns would step down as CEO.[13]

Then came the lawsuits. Three parallel securities fraud complaints argued Nielsen "recklessly disregarded" the impact of GDPR.[14] Barns's company was not the only casualty in the wake of GDPR's implementation; Facebook also was targeted by similar legal action.[15] In fact, a total of eleven comparable class action lawsuits struck companies after the European regulation entered into effect.[16] These complaints sought restitution for companies' poor publicity around data issues, security flaws, or changes in the world of data privacy.[17]

Lessons from GDPR

It's clear that Barns—and Nielsen as a whole—failed in handling GDPR's implementation. Whether by ignorance or deceit, statements he and his team made caused investors to believe the company was more prepared for the regulatory shift than it was.

A key point here is that GDPR and other regulations are more than niche legal issues—they represent whole-of-business risk. Plenty of lawyers knew that GDPR would spur privacy litigation; what many did not expect is that it could also result in securities fraud lawsuits of the sort Nielsen faced. These were not a result of any GDPR violations, but instead targeted Nielsen's preparation (or lack thereof) and how it communicated that preparation, along with the impacts of GDPR on Nielsen's data sources.[18]

Given the growing body of regulations like GDPR and the global nature of many organizations' information technology architectures, it is reasonable to ask, "What do I need to know about data security and privacy laws?" This chapter will answer that question by (1) introducing legal compliance in the context of cybersecurity, (2) explaining the shifting legal landscape, and (3) outlining how your organization can mitigate risks from legal liability and reputational harm.

Why It Matters

When organizations process and store information about their consumers, employees, and business partners, they take on the responsibility of keeping that information safe. All public companies must now consider cybersecurity a major risk factor and declare all "material" cybersecurity incidents. This has significantly increased the level of attention devoted to cyber risk by corporate boards. It might not be possible to reduce the risk of a cyberattack to zero, but an organization can take steps to mitigate the harmful consequences of an attack that results in a data breach or a lack of services.

Cybersecurity is an evolving field, which means that cybersecurity law will continually evolve. This chapter provides background on another component of Embedded Endurance: steps that can be taken to mitigate legal and reputational risks associated with cyberattacks, particularly considering the increasing legal obligations placed upon organizations surrounding cybersecurity. Litigation risk is the possibility that legal action may be taken against an organization. A cyberattack may potentially result in years of legal action and in large financial settlements to compensate for compromises to the individual or collective rights of an organization's customers or clients. Litigation risk may also carry specific consequences for the CEO, depending on the case, and damage the reputation of the firm.

Organizations today must demonstrate to their customers and partners that their information is protected with reasonable care and the services provided to them are secure and reliable. While an organization's precise legal responsibility depends on the geographical region in which it operates, or, potentially, the geographical origins of the data, there are general principles that can be applied to reduce the risk of litigation and reputational harm. Legal responsibilities in the United States primarily relate to matters of data breaches, reflected in the foundational policies, acts, laws, and regulations described in what follows. However, increasingly there are disclosure requirements concerning other types of attacks as well—especially for sectors deemed "critical infrastructure."

Key Concepts

1. Compliance does not guarantee security
2. A dynamic, complex legal landscape
3. Terminology soup: policy, act, law, and regulation

Compliance Does Not Guarantee Security

It is important to keep in mind that complete compliance with cyber frameworks, standards, and laws does not equate to complete security. Despite perfect compliance, protected data and systems may still be at risk. Think of compliance as a necessary step in managing your organization's cyber risk, but one that is ultimately insufficient on its own.

An attack on a major retailer compromising millions of credit card numbers demonstrates the difference between compliance and security. The retailer was certified as compliant with Payment Card Industry (PCI) standards a mere two months before the breach.[19] Nevertheless, the hack occurred. This unfortunate reality emphasizes that compliance should never be the end goal for an organization's cybersecurity program.

A Dynamic, Complex Legal Landscape

Like any other business operation, the collection and processing of information about consumers and business partners are subject to regulation. While it would be impossible to comprehensively explain cyber regulation (the United States alone has dozens of federal statutes with cybersecurity implications), it is important for leaders dealing with cyber risk to understand the general regulatory landscape and the types of obligations imposed, lest you suffer the same consequences that Nielsen did in this chapter's case study. Here we present examples largely from the United States and the European

Union, but the sources of regulation in these examples and their associated categories of obligations have equivalents in most countries.

Basic legal analysis of cybersecurity-related laws must start at the state and local levels of government. In the United States, for example, a firm must consider the privacy and data protection laws of the states in which it operates, since no national-level law exists. Next, leaders must understand the most significant national laws that will drive legal risk analysis. That means an organization must first consider the laws of its home country, followed by other applicable legislation. For example, a German organization must consider German law first, before considering legal risk associated with European Union cybersecurity laws. Cyber law is taking on an increasingly international character, which adds to the complexity of the legal landscape.

The fact that cyber activities often are networked across various jurisdictions adds another degree of complexity. Traditionally, legal compliance for most organizations has meant observing local laws; if a company operates in an area, then it needs to comply with the laws of that area. However, a noticeable trend in data regulation is that national governments have passed laws relating to the data or information of their citizens, which organizations need to follow even if they are not based in that country. With many organizations migrating their networks and data onto cloud services provided by third parties across the globe, it is important that organizations take into consideration the regional regulatory frameworks that affect them based on:

- The physical location of their office(s) or headquarters
- The location in which the business is incorporated
- All the locations served by the business
- The locations where the organization stores individuals' data
- The nationality of the organization's customers

Some regulations will also apply only to certain industries, like financial services or healthcare. Others might only apply to governmental agencies. However, these regulations can still have consequences for private organizations if they contract with governmental agencies. For example, the North American Electric Reliability Corporation (NERC) develops and defines the reliability requirements for operating in the North American power system. The requirements developed by the NERC are then approved by the Federal Energy Regulatory Commission (FERC), which ensures that the standards provided by the NERC are enforced upon all relevant entities within the United States. This enforcement includes imposing monetary sanctions for non-compliance.

Terminology Soup: Policy, Act, Law, and Regulation

The terms "policy," "law," "regulation," and "compliance" are often used interchangeably, but when assessing the level of risk inherent in cybersecurity compliance it's worth distinguishing between policies and laws, in particular (Table 4.1).

Table 4.1 Understanding Compliance Terminology

Understanding Compliance Terminology	
Policies	Outline what a government organization or executive branch aims to achieve, and the procedures and methods it intends to use.
Laws	Passed by Congress or Parliament, laws endow broad policies and principles of legislation with legal force. Laws can only be amended by Congress or Parliament (in the United States, an act is not a law until it is passed by Congress and signed by the president).
Regulations	The implementation guidance of passed laws or by executive order. Regulations are created by federal departments and administrative authorities and directly concern the implementation of a law or executive order. Regulations are legally enforceable if they correspond to appropriate laws. Regulations are subject to amendment or revocation by the executive branch of the government that created them.
Compliance	Defined as fulfilling the official requirements of regulations, acts, laws, and other guidelines.

Going Deeper

State or Provincial Statutes

In analyzing the multiple sources of compliance to adhere to, an organization should begin its analysis at the state or provincial level, and then progress to understanding national and international obligations. In the United States, first understanding state legislation on data breaches and privacy is essential; each state has its own take on data protection laws. It is important that organizations operating in the United States are aware of the different state laws governing cybersecurity incidents as, depending on the state, a breach in cybersecurity may have different implications for how the breach is reported. Beyond data breaches, critical infrastructure has its own sets of state and regional incident reporting requirements, which further complicates the landscape.

Although compliance with these comprehensive regulations may incur additional costs to organizations, these rules form the foundation for recommended cybersecurity practices and therefore mitigate other financial risks.[20] The more an organization can show that it has met standards of cybersecurity—either best practices or explicit state law, even if not in the state of jurisdiction—the stronger the legal argument that the organization has handled its customers' data with reasonable care. If an organization cannot provide evidence of reasonable care in the event of a cybersecurity breach, the cost of litigation will rise very quickly.

Federal or National Statutes

After understanding state- or provincial-level regulations, an organization should then consider applicable federal or national regulations. This type of regulation has the potential to affect entire industries or all companies operating within national or federal boundaries, or affecting a given national citizen population. The United States has enacted statutes that address various aspects of cybersecurity.[21] Some of these are industry-specific, such as the Health Insurance Portability and Accountability Act of 1996 (HIPAA) and the Gramm-Leach-Bliley Act of 1999 (GLBA), while others are geared toward federal agencies, such as the Federal Information Security Management Act of 2002 (FISMA). It is important to note that these statutes were devised decades ago; however, they still function as the foundation for emergent legislation and guidance issued on federal, state, and local levels today.

HIPAA

The Health Insurance Portability and Accountability Act of 1996 requires healthcare entities to protect the confidentiality of healthcare information that can be connected to an identifiable individual. These entities are obliged to take "reasonable and appropriate administrative, technical, and physical safeguards to prevent intentional or unintentional use or disclosure of protected health information" (referred to as PHI).[22] Organizations that do not comply with regulations stipulated by HIPAA are required to pay fines, or may face criminal penalties depending on the severity of the violation.

To avoid the risk of penalty, it is recommended practice to follow up on the HIPAA annual compliance checklist. The checklist includes measures to assist organizations in protecting sensitive information through physical and technical safeguards, as well as an effective data protection strategy.

GLBA

The Gramm-Leach-Bliley Act of 1999 requires financial institutions to protect the security and confidentiality of customers' personal information.[23] This mostly concerns personally identifiable information (PII) and financial information of consumers. The GLBA requires institutions to adhere to several protective measures, including:

- Assigning a designated party for cybersecurity accountability
- Designing, implementing, and monitoring a security assessment program within the organization

- Documenting and proving the effectiveness of these security controls

It is important to note that the GLBA does not apply solely to financial institutions; its extensive interpretation by courts has seen this act applied to organizations that deal with aspects of financing in their own operations. For example, the GLBA is applicable to car dealerships who provide financing to customers for their vehicles, and to real estate appraisers.

As this illustrates, organizations need to understand the legal implications associated with providing certain services (such as financing options for customers), the risks of which may not be apparent from the outset. Leaders in an organization should prioritize consultation with attorneys and cybersecurity experts to better understand these risks. This, in turn, influences what operations and associated resources the organization can afford to prioritize.

Many of the penalties for non-compliance with the GLBA target the organization's leaders. For example, the executive officers (CEO, CIO, etc.) and directors of the organization could pay a fine for each violation, or spend time in prison. The organization will also be liable for financial penalties. The Federal Trade Commission provides further guidance on how to adhere to GLBA regulations.

FISMA
The Federal Information Security Management Act of 2002 applies to private organizations that have contracts with federal agencies, and is principally aimed at upholding the information security of federal agencies. It requires a private contractor to:

- Keep an inventory of its information systems
- Categorize its information into levels of risk to ensure that sensitive information is accorded high protection
- Create security plans and policies[24]

FISMA may be applicable to institutions that receive federal grants, such as NASA, or administer federal loans, such as Medicaid.[25]

Organizations that assist federal agencies in their operations, such as cloud service providers, would also have to comply with FISMA.[26]

FISMA provides annual evaluations on all federal agencies based on their compliance with FISMA laws. The results of the evaluations are made publicly available, meaning that organizations could face the following repercussions:

- Reputational damage due to media coverage of a low evaluation score.
- As the scores are available to the public, hackers use this knowledge to identify organizations with poor IT security. This may result in security breaches.
- As the result of a low score, organizations may also have their budgets reduced by the White House Office of Management and Budget (OMB).[27]

The General Data Protection Regulation

The Nielsen case study centers on the European Union's General Data Protection Regulation, which is another example of far-reaching cybersecurity regulation akin to national or federal regulation. The GDPR is an example of cyber law that applies to businesses even if they do not have a physical presence within the EU.

The GDPR applies to:

- Organizations based in the EU that process the personal data of natural persons
- Organizations that do not have a branch in the EU but which offer goods and services to individuals residing in the EU and which process the personal data of EU residents[28]

It's helpful to understand some useful terminology. The GDPR defines the above-mentioned terms as follows:

- Personal data refers to "any information relating to an identified or identifiable natural person."[29]
- Processing of personal data includes "collection, recording, organization, structuring, storage, adaptation or alteration, retrieval, consultation, use, disclosure by transmission, dissemination or otherwise making available, alignment or combination, restriction, erasure or destruction."[30]

If an organization meets these requirements, various obligations can be imposed. Some of the most pertinent obligations are covered in the following paragraphs.

Data Subject Rights

The GDPR gives individuals rights over their data, such as a right to access data and a "right to be forgotten." For example, a user can ask an organization to provide all the data it holds that may be used to identify the user. Organizations may also be required to give users clear information about how their data will be used.[31] It additionally obliges organizations to implement appropriate technical safeguards and breach notification requirements.

Processing and Controlling of Data

As the GDPR regulates the processing of personal data, it imposes obligations on the "controllers" and "processors" of that data. Since the relationship between a controller (a person or organization who controls how data is processed) and a processor (an organization that processes data on behalf of the controller) is often based on a third-party contract, these obligations will be dealt with in the section on third-party risks.

Breach Notification and Incident Response

In the event of a breach that compromises the rights of individuals' data, a supervisory body will need to be notified if the breach is likely to have a serious negative effect on individuals, such as exposing them to identify theft, reputational damage, or financial loss. This needs to be done within seventy-two hours of the organization becoming aware of the breach.[32]

Penalties for Non-Compliance

Because the GDPR gives data rights to individuals, it allows individuals to claim compensation from companies that did not comply with the GDPR's requirements. It also empowers supervisory authorities to impose heavy administrative fines for certain kinds of non-compliance (such as not acquiring sufficient consent when processing a child's information, or not having implemented appropriate technical safeguards).[33] Breaching the requirement to implement technical safeguards can make an organization liable for fines, or even a percentage of its worldwide annual turnover.

Overall, the GDPR's requirements pose significant questions about how an organization may need to reprioritize its business operations and resources, and what measures it needs to implement in its cyber risk mitigation strategy.

Regulations Developed by Governmental Agencies

HIPAA, GLBA, and FISMA are examples of laws that were passed by the United States Congress and which have the status of federal law. An organization's legal obligations can have multiple sources, however, and not all legal regulation comes directly from Congress or parliamentary bodies. Some regulations are developed by non-parliamentary governmental agencies.

The U.S. Securities and Exchange Commission

A prominent example of regulation of this kind is the disclosure requirements of the U.S. Securities and Exchange Commission (SEC), a federal agency that enforces federal securities law and regulates the securities industry.

The SEC has treated cyber breaches within the framework of pre-existing regulations, such as those relating to the disclosure of information about publicly listed companies. Similar to the regulations described in the previous sections, the SEC requires organizations to disclose cyber incidents or associated risks and events "that a reasonable investor would consider important to an investment decision."[34] Non-compliance with SEC disclosure requirements can result in significant financial penalties.[35] Along with highlighting the reputational damage of delaying or avoiding disclosure, the SEC requirements further illustrate the need for organizations to treat cybersecurity as a major risk factor, and the need to ensure the timely and accurate disclosure of incidents.

Federal Energy Regulatory Commission

Another example of cyber regulations developed by governmental agencies is the compliance framework that the US Federal Energy Regulatory Commission mandates. Of particular interest is the North American Electric Reliability Corporation Critical Infrastructure Protection (NERC CIP) compliance framework. It is a set of requirements aimed at managing the cyber risk in North America's electric grid.[36]

As mentioned earlier in this chapter, NERC develops the reliability requirements for power operators, and FERC enforces them. Some examples of NERC CIP standards subject to FERC enforcement include provisions for personnel and training, incident reporting and response planning, security management controls, and electronic security perimeters, among others.[37] Note that every standard is far more than a single checkbox requirement; rather, each has its own host of sub-requirements and implementation assessment details, both of which can be extensive. As was the case for SEC regulations, FERC non-compliance can also carry financial penalties.

Non-Regulatory Standards

Non-governmental industry bodies can also develop standards that may or may not be backed up with contractual sanctions in the event of non-compliance (such as financial penalties for breach of contract, or no longer being able to accept credit cards as a payment option). These standards matter not only because of possible contractual penalties, but also because they can inform industry recommended practices. These recommended practices could ultimately be adopted to mitigate legal liability and reputational harm. However, as explained earlier, compliance doesn't guarantee cybersecurity incidents won't occur.

An example of contractual-sanction-backed standards is the Payment Card Industry Data Security Standard (DSS). The PCI Data Security Council was founded by leading credit card companies to develop security standards for card account data. A merchant that wishes to enable payment using these card brands would have to comply with the council's data security standards or face fines or revocation of the privilege of accepting payment by credit card.[38] These standards are sometimes adopted by governments in their own regulations. The PCI DSS has been adopted by several U.S. states in their own laws, for example.[39]

Taking Action

Legal liability and the need for compliance are clearly important, as this chapter's case study illustrates. Data breaches and other cyberattacks can result in heavy financial losses and reputational harm, not to mention damages to individuals. Given that it is impossible to reduce the risk of an incident to zero, here are some actionable ways to minimize compliance risk.

Adopting a Cybersecurity Framework

Cybersecurity frameworks provide plans for securing the confidentiality, availability, and integrity of sensitive data, and regulate access to critical information systems and networks. They also provide guidance on directing sufficient resources toward processes that support an organization's cybersecurity objectives.[40]

The dominant cybersecurity framework adopted to address the aspects of cyber threats faced by various industry sectors is created by the National Institute of Standards and Technology (NIST).[41]

The NIST Cybersecurity Framework is a prominent framework that has seen widespread use across many sectors. The NIST framework was developed to provide a standard set of methodologies and procedures to guide organizations in assessing their capacity to effectively mitigate cyberattacks.

Help your organization adopt a security framework by finding one that suits its unique needs based on its sector and organizational context. Use the NIST Cybersecurity Framework as a launching point, compare alternatives, and even consider creating your own framework by combining or adapting those that already exist to better suit your needs. Consult different members of your organization in this process, since a given framework can have disparate impacts on different business units. Of course, simply deciding on a framework is just one step. While the frameworks themselves have useful implementation pointers, there is a plethora of reading materials and organizations that specifically focus on implementing such frameworks that could be consulted to help guide your organization.

Build a Cyber Policy/Act/Law/ Regulation "Watch List"

Cybersecurity policies, acts, laws, and regulations are evolving within each major sector and across various levels of governments. It is helpful for leadership to familiarize themselves with relevant cybersecurity guidance and maintain a "watch list" for continued updates to these. By doing so, the organization will not be blindsided by adjustments to policies, acts, laws, and regulations. Instead, it can actively manage compliance risk according to relevant changes.

Equally important is tuning in to various agencies and governing bodies that may be issuing such updates. Such agencies are often eager to engage with organizations seeking guidance on compliance and welcome inquiries accordingly. In some cases, it may be wise to build direct lines of communication and relationships with these authoritative groups.

Purchase Cyber Insurance

Cybersecurity incidents almost always introduce new litigation risk to your organization. While the management of litigation risk is nuanced, insurance can transfer some of the financial risk to an insurer, lowering the overall risk profile for the organization.

Cybersecurity insurance can significantly bolster your company's ability to weather such lawsuits financially, and in some cases it may be the difference between an organization remaining in business or closing shop.

Financial losses resulting from a breach have various sources, such as the costs of notifying affected parties, legal fees, compensation for affected individuals, and regulatory fines. Insurance coverage usually divides these sources of loss into three categories:

1. Liability (such as compensating others for their losses)
2. Breach response (such as notification costs)
3. Fines (for not complying with regulations)

It is vital to know what kinds of losses the insurance covers and what triggers the insurance. The organization would need to know whether civil penalties (imposed by governmental agencies for violations) are covered, for example, and whether it would be covered even if it had been negligent.[42]

Insurance companies have developed two types of cyber insurance to address the growing need for coverage from attacks: first-party coverage and third-party coverage.

First-Party and Third-Party Coverage

First-party coverage insures an organization against its own losses from cyberattacks. Third-party coverage, conversely, insures a company against cyberattack damages to other entities (third parties) for which the company bears some responsibility. For example, an IT company could be sued by a client over a cyberattack the client suffered, and third-party coverage might insure the IT company against this fallout.

Reimbursable Expenses

The following table lists the reimbursable expenses typically covered by cybersecurity insurance (Table 4.2).

Given the complexity of the compliance landscape coupled with the complexity of the threat landscape, an organization's leadership should consult with reputable cybersecurity insurance brokers

Table 4.2 Reimbursable Expenses

Reimbursable Expenses	
Forensic investigations of cybersecurity events	After a data breach or similar event, preventing future events depends on a thorough understanding of how the event occurred. This may involve contracting a third-party security firm, or, increasingly, coordination with federal or national law enforcement agencies.
Extortion	Cyber extortion methods like ransomware can create significant financial risk for the organization. Other forms of extortion that may be covered include blackmail through the accessing of confidential information.
Costs due to notification of privacy breaches	The notification requirements introduced by laws and regulations such as the GDPR may carry significant penalties if not complied with, but even perfect compliance can be costly. Additional costs may also be incurred through communication with affected parties, or monitoring the credit or other information of customers who are affected by the breach.
Reputational losses	Insuring against reputational harm is also fundamentally a matter of recovering some of the financial costs associated with reputational damage control. The costs of reputation management should not be overlooked as one of the costs of a cyberattack. Organizations will need to fund a communications team to pursue reputational damage control through various media platforms, such as social media and print media.
Business losses	These are losses incurred by business operational downtime due to a cybersecurity event—for example, sale losses by a large e-commerce store while a breach is being investigated. Data loss and the costs of data recovery may also be included in these financial losses.[*]

[*] Lindros, K., and E. Tittel. 2016. "What Is Cyber Insurance and Why You Need It." CIO. https://www.csoonline.com/article/3065474/what-is-cyber-insurance-and-why-you-need-it.html.

to acquire coverage that adequately covers both the risks posed by regulatory compliance and those posed by evolving cyber threats.[43] Brokers should focus on addressing any coverage gaps as well as achieving premiums that make financial sense given the risk profile of the organization.

Brokers may opt for cybersecurity insurers that offer additional risk management services, such as:

- **Private arbitration services:** Private arbitration allows settlements to be handled with limited publicity, mitigating reputational harm. Private arbitration can also limit other legal costs by avoiding court proceedings, thereby saving time and money.
- **Penetration testing, simulated cyberattacks, and other security checks:** Insurance providers may probe the organization's networks and systems for common vulnerabilities as well as vulnerabilities particular to their industry (for example, routes to gain access to PHI in the healthcare industry). This testing enables organizations to adjust their cybersecurity plans and priorities that may currently be exposing them to litigation risk as well as financial and reputational risk.
- **Response management:** After a cyber attack, there is much to do. Stakeholders need to be informed, otherwise dormant processes need to be activated, reporting for compliance purposes is necessary, and extensive documentation is required to demonstrate that the incident was properly managed. Some insurers work with third-party providers who facilitate this process, providing assurance to the company and its stakeholders that procedures and compliance requirements were handled appropriately in the wake of an incident.

Beyond Cyber Insurance

It is important to understand the array of insurance policies your organizations subscribe to and how each may relate to cyber incidents. Beyond purchasing explicit cyber insurance, there may be what is called "silent cover" in other types of insurance policies your organization holds that may cover damages or help in light of a cyberattack. Such a policy may include business continuity insurance, which could possibly cover losses experienced when services are down due to a ransomware attack. Each policy, underwritten by different insurers, will have different coverage and exclusions, so it is critical to understand the coverage details for your organization's various policies and how each can be valuable in light of an attack.

Action on the Front Lines

The responsibility for exhibiting Embedded Endurance leadership extends all the way to the top, as the fate of the Nielsen CEO demonstrates. Prior to GDPR's entry into force, Dwight Barns should have worked to better understand and communicate the full impact the legal regime would have on his organization.

We recognize this can be difficult, given the unprecedented nature of so many cyber frameworks, standards, and laws. But as Barns's story illustrates, both your organization and your own job security depend on it.

A meeting of the minds among cyber stakeholders, including insurers, organizations, and regulatory bodies, is ultimately critical when it comes to evaluating the aftermath of a cyber attack. To achieve this alignment, other industries have adopted a standard of care, which helps to clarify how organizations should act and what they are to be held responsible for after an incident.

Cyber Crossroads, an effort to outline a standard of care for cyber, was co-led by Falco, who acted as the principal investigator for the project.[44] The cyber standard of care builds on tenants of other professional standards of care (such as in medicine) and outlines a process for organizations to conduct cyber risk planning as an ongoing exercise. The project was sponsored by leading cyber insurance companies and credit rating agencies, where the launch event for the report was headlined by representatives from the U.S. Securities and Exchange Commission and the United Kingdom's Department for Digital, Culture, Media and Sport, which speaks to the need for an organization to align their cyber strategy with the expectations of a broad range of stakeholders. The Embedded Endurance strategy offers an approach to meet this proposed standard of care.

Main Takeaway

The financial and reputational costs associated with legal non-compliance alone justify making cyber risk management part of an organization's Embedded Endurance strategy. This includes the mitigation of risks associated with legal compliance. To manage the risks related to cybersecurity and the law, executives need to acquaint themselves with the various sources of legal obligations and industry standards, such as state law, federal law, and industry bodies, and adopt a business strategy that mitigates the financial and reputational risks associated with legal compliance. Even if it is impossible to reduce the risk of a data breach to zero, an organization can still attempt to meet its legal obligations and be able to show that it treated information about its customers, employees, or stakeholders with reasonable care.

5

Who Is Responsible for Cybersecurity?

Cyber risk prevention and resilience is not a one-person show—it takes a village

Case Study

In September 2017, news quickly spread that Equifax—one of America's "Big Three" credit reporting agencies—had suffered a cyberattack that compromised the personal information of almost half the country.

The entire nation was asking, "Who's to blame?"

What Happened?

In May 2017, attackers breached Equifax and surveilled its network undetected for over seventy days.[1] During this time, the hackers stole personal data for nearly half the American population from almost fifty separate databases that Equifax had largely collected without the public's knowledge or consent.[2]

By the time Equifax detected and blocked further data exfiltration in late July, the hackers had stolen personal information including the names and social security numbers of almost 150 million Americans.[3] Also snagged were addresses and driver's license information for tens of millions, as well as credit card information

Confronting Cyber Risk. Gregory Falco and Eric Rosenbach, Oxford University Press. © Oxford University Press 2022. DOI: 10.1093/oso/9780197526545.003.0005

for over 200,000 more.[4] Exacerbating the catastrophe, the company botched its incident response: the website assisting victims crashed, output false results, and suffered its own data security gaffes, among other issues.[5]

The resulting legal settlement alone cost Equifax at least $575 million, although that bill could swell to $700 million.[6]

Thus, the question of who was to blame weighed heavily on the minds of everyone from average Americans to Washington politicians.

Who's Responsible?

At first, the answer to the question of who was responsible seemed simple enough. CEO Richard Smith largely blamed Graeme Payne, senior vice president and chief information officer for global corporate platforms, for not forwarding an email about the vulnerability to the IT staff member who needed to manually apply the patch.[7]

It does not take a lawyer to recognize this view of culpability as narrow. If he had instead adopted an Embedded Endurance perspective on cybersecurity, Smith would have recognized a host of additional failures that contributed to the catastrophe.

For starters, any update protocol requiring a senior VP to personally forward patch notices to specific engineers should be a red flag. Payne was one of over 400 employees who received the email, and he believed he was copied on it solely for informational purposes. Contrary to Smith's argument, Payne testified that Equifax's patch management policy did not require him to take action on the message. Furthermore, the company did not have redundancies within its patching process to verify that all proper individuals were notified.[8]

But the systemic issues ran deeper. The network monitoring technology that should have detected the intrusion had been inactive for nineteen months. In fact, it was only when Equifax belatedly updated this system in July that it noticed the suspicious activity.[9]

Finally, Smith had pursued an aggressive acquisition-driven growth strategy in his decade leading the company. As Equifax cobbled together a variety of custom legacy systems, the company's IT environment became particularly complex and difficult to manage.[10]

Preparing You to Succeed

When viewed from this systems perspective, Equifax's cyber crisis was less a matter of "if" and more a matter of "when." Further, the responsibility was not solely that of the chief information officer for global corporate platforms, as cited by the CEO, but instead a wide swath of senior leaders. This is most clearly demonstrated by the fact that Smith ultimately retired as CEO under pressure resulting from the breach.

The potential scale of cybersecurity failures should be sufficient to motivate organizations to adopt this systems approach. As bad as the Equifax hack was, Yahoo set the world record for the largest known breach when it disclosed that an attack in 2013 had affected all 3 billion of its user accounts.[11] Verizon—which was acquiring Yahoo at the time—responded by cutting $350 million from its original acquisition offer.[12]

This chapter tackles a broader version of the question on everyone's mind in the wake of the Equifax and Yahoo hacks: "Who is responsible for cybersecurity?" It dives into (1) leadership roles in cybersecurity governance and (2) cybersecurity awareness and training. Through these pages, you will learn how your organization can better shoulder the responsibility of preventing an Equifax-style disaster.

Why It Matters

Organizations typically identify dedicated individuals or "champions" to hold various responsibilities related to the organization's security. Champions can include anyone from line managers who would like to lead the charge to senior management such as the CEO, CIO, and CISO who are evangelizing security issues across senior management. A security champion is generally different from the person who is ultimately accountable for cybersecurity risk management, referred to as an accountable officer.[13] The individual assigned as the accountable officer should be someone responsible for the organization's performance, considering that cyber risk ultimately impacts all aspects of the organization. Therefore, the role of accountable officer fits squarely with the organization's CEO or equivalent. Cyber risk is a major leadership issue, as cyber risk is business risk. Should the most powerful individual in the organization not be leading the charge on cyber risk (and be assigned consequences when cyber events occur under their watch), it will not be perceived as a top priority. Should the CEO not willfully embrace this accountability, it may be bestowed on them anyway by stakeholders and the board of the directors, as we saw was the case for Equifax, where the CEO was forced out as a result of the breach.

While accountability should sit with the CEO, from an operational perspective the embedding of cyber risk endurance is the responsibility of all senior leadership. Senior leaders cannot be at all places at all times to keep a watchful eye on cyber risk; therefore, a strong governance program should be established to manage cybersecurity risk and, in doing so, protect the interests of the organization's stakeholders. Cybersecurity governance requires strategic direction, commitment, and transparent reporting within and outside of the organization.

The Direct Benefits of a Strong Governance Program

It may be easy to create the impression of a robust defense when utilizing perfect information system architecture, top-of-the-range tools, and technical best practices. However, this chapter's case study is a reminder that it is essential to support cybersecurity programs with a strong governance program to ensure that cyber risk mitigation strategies permeate all levels of an organization.

To sufficiently address the security of information systems, good governance of cybersecurity programs aims to:

- Strategically align cybersecurity efforts with business strategies to support organization objectives
- Support risk management by enforcing necessary controls to mitigate risks
- Reduce the impact of security breaches on information resources
- Improve resource management by efficiently managing cybersecurity knowledge and infrastructure[14]

Some of the broader benefits of effective governance, with a focus on risk mitigation, include:

- Increased predictability of business operations
- Greater control over the confidentiality, integrity, and availability of data, resulting in less potential for civil or legal liability
- More cost-effective allocation of security resources
- Improvements in risk management, business process, and effective incident response in the case of a breach
- The ability to make critical decisions based on clear, valid information
- Greater safeguarding of sensitive information during important business activities, such as acquisitions and mergers, regulatory responses, and business process recovery

Key Concepts

1. Accountable leadership
2. Enterprise security policy
3. Cybersecurity culture

Accountable Leadership

It should not take a cyber expert to recognize that Equifax CEO Richard Smith's failures leading up to the hack—and especially his abrogation of responsibility in its aftermath—demonstrated extremely poor leadership. Despite his efforts to push the culpability upon his subordinates, the majority of the blame sits upon his shoulders.

Given that digital technologies are essential to every major private and public organization today, the idea that the CEO is ultimately responsible for managing cyber risk would seem uncontroversial. Unfortunately, in our conversations and consultations with CEOs around the globe, we have found that top executives continue to treat cybersecurity as a second-tier obligation better handled by IT engineers.

Let us be clear: the CEO is ultimately responsible for cybersecurity. This remains true even if the organization has a dedicated CISO, CIO, or analogous cyber risk champion. Does the presence of a CFO absolve the CEO of responsibility for a company's financial performance? Certainly not. In the modern world cyber risk literacy is "core curriculum" for top leadership. By a similar token, the board of directors has a fiduciary duty to ensure that the CEO is executing on cyber risk priorities.

Operationally, the board of directors may not have day-to-day oversight of the organization, but given their fiduciary duty to shareholders and the cyber risk implications for a business, they must be actively engaged in conversations with leadership on the matter. As part of a board's fiduciary duty, it is critical for someone on the board to be knowledgeable about cyber risk. They need to be asking questions on the current state of risk and ensure that a cyber governance process is operating as intended. Board members are also accountable for cyber risk, which is reflected in their purchasing of directors and officers (D&O) insurance that often explicitly covers their liability in the case of cyber disruption.

Accountable leadership sits atop this chapter's "Key Concepts" list because it is foundational to the ideas that follow. An organization's enterprise security policy will make a significant difference only if top leadership prioritizes it. This is especially true given the nature of cyber risk management: the impact on the bottom line may be difficult for shortsighted leaders to envision until it is too late. The data breach cost Equifax hundreds of millions of dollars. Furthermore, buy-in from top leadership is critical for establishing a strong cybersecurity culture. If the CEO does not take personal responsibility for managing cyber risk, do not expect a midlevel manager to do so.

Enterprise Security Policy

Every organization, regardless of industry, requires an enterprise security policy (ESP) that outlines the various roles and responsibilities for both IT and OT security to ensure effective cybersecurity. The ESP should include guidance on policy implementation and maintenance as well as the responsibilities of end users (who may be employees or customers, depending on the organization). The ESP may be casually referred to as the organization's "security program policy."[15]

The ESP must reflect and support the organization's mission and strategic objectives, as well as the role of security in achieving them. Leadership's co-creation of and buy-in to the ESP are absolutely critical. This includes constant involvement of the general counsel, who is generally responsible for corporate governance and keeping the organization aligned with laws and regulations.

The ESP is an executive-level document, meaning that it would not be accessed by most employees but rather used as the foundation on which to draft policies that cascade down the organizational hierarchy. The ESP broadly outlines policies and specifies channels and mechanisms for accountability in the organization's Embedded Endurance approach, including which executives are accountable for which aspects of the overall security program. The ESP does not require frequent updating, as could issue-specific security policies (ISSPs), such as the description of appropriate internet use, and system-specific policies (SysSPs), such as documentation on appropriate firewall configurations. An organization will only have one ESP, which incorporates all the necessary components, but it would have several ISSPs and SysSPs, depending on the structure of its information systems.

Think of an ESP as an outline of your organization's core security principles and best practices. Your ESP will inform the policies that relate to technical as well as non-technical subcategories. It may also cover topics such as building a cybersecurity budget, evaluating vendors for their security practices, and cybersecurity talent management.

Cybersecurity Culture

High-level aspects of the organization's plans to develop its cybersecurity culture will be outlined in the ESP and corresponding subpolicies. However, a cybersecurity culture does not simply emerge merely because policies and procedures are clearly outlined. Instead, leaders must make clear through their actions that cybersecurity is essential to the organization's mission.

For an example of what *not* to do, examine the Equifax case study described earlier in this chapter. When the information of almost 150 million people was leaked, Equifax's CEO responded by attempting to deflect blame onto a software provider, Apache Struts, for vulnerabilities found in their web server. However, Apache Struts maintains that a patch was made available to fix the vulnerability. The CEO of Equifax then shifted the blame to Graeme Payne, the senior vice president and chief information officer for global corporate platforms, for not forwarding an email about the vulnerability to the IT staff member who, according to the CEO, failed to apply the patch. Equifax's handling of the data breach has widely been cited as a poor example of embodying effective cybersecurity culture.[16]

There are five principles behind a strong cybersecurity culture:

1. Transparency
2. Accountability
3. Appropriate system knowledge

4. Compliance with policy and procedure
5. Formal communication channels

In the majority of cybersecurity breaches, one or more of the five principles outlined above has not been sufficiently applied. These principles start and end with high-quality management practices, and aim to limit the impact of the human factor on cyber risk management.

Going Deeper

Cybersecurity Culture Principles

Transparency
While transparency is not always the silver bullet it is touted to be for all management issues, in the case of cyber risk management, regular open and honest communication is essential to creating a robust cybersecurity culture.

Practically, transparency within an organization's cybersecurity culture translates to the following actions: having no delays in error reporting; emphasizing the importance of reporting; defining the consequences of unreported issues; updating protocols, policies, and procedures; and having open discussions on mistakes, failures, and successes.

Of course, the development of a culture of transparency around cybersecurity within the organization is not automatic. Instead, it depends heavily on the adherence of leadership to the principles of early and effective incident reporting, and rewarding reporting rather than implicitly rewarding omission.

If the organization does not report its cybersecurity breaches as per regulation and best practice, or if it does not consistently act with transparency, initiatives to improve this aspect among its employees will ultimately ring hollow. As with all management practices, adherence to both policy and principle must be practiced at all levels of the organization to have the desired impact.

In the age of engaging artificial intelligence for a variety of security functions, transparency is not only a matter of willpower. Some AI architectures such as deep neural networks are "black box" decision models, meaning they do not allow humans to easily understand how they make decisions. In fact, an entire research subfield has sprung up around the topic of explainable AI, with researchers puzzling over subcomponents of this problem at annual gatherings.

While the notion of (un-)explainable AI may at first seem abstract, it can present very real problems for your organization. First, transparency is a crucial tool in the fight to keep your AI algorithms performing at their best. Rarely are AI systems a set-it-and-forget-it matter in the real world, as their performance often degrades with time if not maintained properly. Second, AI algorithms can replicate and magnify bias. Visibility into these systems can prevent your organization from using a tool that discriminates against protected groups, and would be important for any audit or legal investigation that arises. Third, transparency is a critical tool in the defense against attacks. AI systems are vulnerable to a swath of hacks that both include and extend beyond "regular" cyberattacks.

Transparency in AI systems is therefore important to inform troubleshooting, provide ethical and legal guidance, and detect cyberattacks. Detailed logs of a model's performance, as well as audit trails for any data fed to the model throughout its lifetime, are essential in this effort.[17]

Accountability

Accountability is a fundamental aspect of Embedded Endurance, and refers to the idea that each individual who relies on an information system to accomplish their role is responsible for upholding the policies and procedures that protect the security of that information system. However, many organizations have displayed signs of a widening "accountability gap," with 40 percent of executives admitting that they do not feel responsible for dealing with the consequences of a cyberattack, and that such a responsibility should fall on the IT or security team.[18]

Much of the concern around accountability in organizations can be attributed to a lack of cybersecurity awareness among leaders.[19] Bridging the accountability gap is thus a matter of shifting the responsibility back to executives by equipping them with the awareness necessary to accept accountability for keeping information systems secure. Below is an overview of the steps organizations can take to improve their leaders' cyber awareness:

- **Train all leaders in cyber literacy:** The first step in closing the accountability gap is to train those in leadership positions to interpret the results of security reports. This includes keeping leaders updated on cyber terminology.
- **Make leaders aware of the implications of a breach:** Executives should be regularly updated with information about the most current types of threats and the potential harm that threats may cause.
- **Ensure that leaders are briefed on compliance policies:** Organizations have to consider their adherence to national and international cybersecurity policies to avoid legal and compliance risks.[20]

Appropriate System Knowledge

It would be neither feasible nor fair to expect every employee, or even every manager, to have any depth of knowledge about systems outside their own work. However, most employees currently have a practically negligible degree of knowledge about the critical assets that are essential to their work, and how data is shared and processed in their daily tasks. Without at least some base understanding of how systems, networks, and data support their business, employees cannot be expected to use their intuition to identify errors or suspicious activity within the information system.

It is therefore important that cybersecurity awareness and training, as expanded on later in this chapter, provides individuals with the tools they need to better understand the critical assets they are most frequently in contact with. Extra care must be taken for newer systems or for systems with increased complexity, such as cloud infrastructure. Specific individuals within each department or role may require more in-depth training than their peers to bolster the overall understanding of the shared systems within the group.

Critically, information systems are not static objects to be studied and understood once, but are in constant flux in most organizations. Managers must therefore be aware of any changes to the systems used within their department(s), and push for additional training where required. Appropriate policy also needs to be drafted to ensure that functional and departmental managers appreciate their role in measuring and reporting on the effectiveness of systems training.

The need for all employees—regardless of their technical insight and skill—to apply a critical mindset to cybersecurity follows the need for adequate system knowledge. A culture of questioning may appear to contravene a culture that closely follows policy and procedure, but these are not contradictory; rather, employees who apply a critical eye to their work are more likely to spot and report issues and errors and, therefore, support the practice of following procedures.

In order to create a cybersecurity culture in which individuals are encouraged to apply critical thinking to their activities (and those of others), a questioning attitude must be rewarded appropriately and emphasized during training.

The integrity of an organization's cybersecurity culture and policies must also be open to questioning. Individual employees should not only be encouraged to flag system issues and thoroughly check their work and operating procedures, but also should be encouraged to point out oversights and outdated information in policies and procedures. When this behavior is encouraged and rewarded (and effectively managed), it creates a cybersecurity culture in which individuals take accountability for maintaining effective cybersecurity operations at a high level—and not only in their own work.

Compliance with Policy and Procedure

Policies and procedures may be drafted flawlessly, but they are useless if not enforced. As part of awareness and training initiatives, every individual employee should become aware of where to find policies and procedures that relate to their work and role. They should also have a clear understanding of whom they can speak with if there are any questions about these policies and procedures.

Once training has been provided, regular operations must also include inspections to ensure compliance with policies, and retraining should be undertaken where required. Every department or function must have one designated individual who is accountable for making sure that employees comply with policies. Accountability here must include not only observing day-to-day individual compliance, but also reporting on changes required to policy or procedure.

Formal Communication Channels

Establishing formal communication channels and policies not only ensures that information is communicated to those who have the power to act on it, but further supports principles of transparency and policy compliance.

It is important for leadership to appreciate the importance of establishing and adhering to formal communication channels for cybersecurity concerns even *outside* of pure incident management.

A basic communication strategy should outline and specify the following within appropriate policy:[21]

- An intradepartmental communication strategy for issue reporting (for example, a formal channel for reporting an issue on a local system to an appropriate functional or departmental manager, and outlining clear expectations for that manager's actions following the report)
- Escalation procedures for reporting departmental and functional system issues, as well as overall information system issues
- An escalation policy for urgent error reporting or anomaly detection
- At least two formal channels for each of the above occurrences, which simultaneously ensures that there is increased oversight on report handling and leaders are held accountable for reporting and responding to the concerns raised by individuals,

and reduces the chances that an error goes unaddressed within an appropriate window of time
- In the case of a confirmed compromise, depending on its nature, the strategy must include tactics for communication with both internal and external stakeholders and any relevant federal or regulatory bodies

Budgeting and Resource Allocation

The effective leadership of a cyber risk program requires thoughtful budgeting and resource allocation. Here we highlight three aspects of budgeting and resource allocation that play important roles in executing effective cyber risk mitigation strategies—namely, advocating for adequate funding, return on investment (ROI), and metrics and measurable effectiveness.

Advocating for Adequate Funding

Creating a budget for a cybersecurity program can be difficult because of the challenge of articulating how additional expenditures will lower risk. Managers and program owners thus often find themselves with the difficult task of advocating for a budget to a skeptical audience.

Each organization needs to consider the threats that they are most vulnerable to, so that they can prioritize their mitigation resources to address the most impactful risks urgently and comprehensively. Lacking sufficient funds and resources to mitigate cyber risk could be among your cyber leadership's greatest challenges in achieving these goals.[22]

In many cases where organizations do attempt to budget for cyber risk mitigation, essential mitigation needs are buried in the organization's larger IT budget, as projects and upgrades tend to provide more obvious value. However, it is important that organizations develop a specific budget for cyber risk mitigation to ensure that enough resources are available to protect critical cyber assets from threat actors.

The involvement of management and understanding of the importance of cyber risk resources is, therefore, crucial. While there is no magic number for a security budget, we have personally seen values anywhere from 2 to 10 percent of total IT spending. Organizations that are in the process of implementing large programs to improve cyber risk management are generally found to have increased their cybersecurity budget recently and significantly. While cybersecurity budgets may be increasing, many organizations still do not dedicate enough consideration to direct cyber risk management expenditures. It is even appropriate to budget a percentage of total IT spending to the cyber governance process itself.

Making compelling arguments for mitigating business risk through managing cyber risk provides a strong basis for requesting increased funding for cybersecurity. Some compelling arguments include the following:

- Requests for cybersecurity budget can be substantiated through direct reference to the main types of risk and to the potential impact of compromise of each inventoried information asset.
- Reference can be made to recent case studies, which provide undeniable cautionary tales that illustrate the true impact of lax cybersecurity management.
- Emphasis can be placed on the need for cybersecurity to be an ongoing effort that pervades the organization's attitudes to asset management, rather than a delegated department or one-time sprint.

It is also necessary for cybersecurity representatives to approach executive management by focusing on the terms that they are already familiar with in decisions that affect business systems: return on investment and risk.

Reframing IT and OT security spending as an asset in itself can also be a valuable tool in securing the resources necessary to bolster a cyber risk mitigation program.

Return on Mitigation

Executives and boards often find themselves with the task of carefully evaluating the return on investment of an expenditure, as investment in one aspect or department must sometimes translate to lower investments in others. Given the difficulties of fully grasping the evolving importance of IT and OT security and cyber risk mitigation, and the reputation of cybersecurity as a "grudge expense," reframing investment IT and OT security in terms that are familiar to business decision-making has the potential to change the outcome of budget deliberations.

When advocating for greater investment in cyber risk mitigation, it is helpful to refer to return on mitigation (ROM) as the primary indicator for the required shift in resource allocation. ROM can be determined by comparing the cost of mitigation investments with the monetary impact of compromise to each information asset. In other words, ROM would focus on how much would *not* be lost if effective mitigation was in place—thus reframing the potential losses of risk as business gains.

Although it is possible to focus solely on the financial benefit of cybersecurity investment, this is not always recommended. The reason for this is that the financial impact of a cyber breach might be difficult to ascertain. For example, perhaps an attacker has accessed your system but has not stolen anything, as occasionally happens when adversaries are found to have access to complex control systems such as the U.S. electric grid.[23] Fortunately, such hackers often do not act on their access; rather, they are present for psychological leverage or in case a cyber counterstrike is required. It is not clear what financial value can be assigned to this unsettling fact. Further, reputational damage is among the most damaging effects of a breach. The impact on this intangible asset will not necessarily be clear, as there are many variables that must be factored in to evaluate the effect on reputation. In cases such as this, you might want to redefine how to think about the appropriate metric for return. It does not always have to be financially oriented.

Metrics and Measurable Effectiveness

Business gain on cybersecurity investments is not a useful concept unless it is measured and reported on regularly and as accurately as possible. For IT and OT improvements to be quantified and budgets to be adjusted in accordance with performance, reporting procedures must be clear and prioritized across relevant policies and role expectations. Where possible, policies should also define appropriate metrics for measuring improvement to vulnerabilities by investing in controls.

The cybersecurity program champion, whether that be the CEO, the CISO, a committee, or another representative, must devise a schedule for regular feedback concerning cybersecurity progress, risks mitigated, and changes to the cyberthreat landscape that may necessitate internal budget adjustments.

Regular, participative evaluation and transparent communication among upper management concerning cybersecurity have become essential not only to digital resilience, but also to overall business strategy, and it should be prioritized appropriately. These are essential to growing the maturity of each business process as well. The more mature a process or program, the more its effectiveness is improved and the greater its business impact.

Categories of Measurement

The effectiveness of cybersecurity efforts, and therefore return on investment on allocation to cybersecurity budgets, cannot be determined without comprehensive measurement. The National Institute of Standards and Technology advises that the following three types of measurement or metric be included in every cybersecurity strategy:[24]

1. Implementation measures
2. Effectiveness and efficiency measures
3. Impact measures

Implementation Measures

Implementation measures apply directly to processes and security controls. This includes immature processes that have not undergone extensive and repeated evaluation over time, and which may still be adjusted relatively regularly.[25] Efficiency and impact measures are applied to more mature processes. Some overlap does exist between these measures.

Implementation measures are used to report on the organization's adherence to its specific IT and OT security policies, ultimately tracking back to the ESP (for example, measuring what percentage of systems are operating within approved password policies). The organization may start with this metric at 60 percent and gradually build toward 100 percent.

Given their direct application in day-to-day operations, it is not unusual for implementation measures to be associated with stringent deadlines (for example, for all systems to comply with password policies within twenty-one business days). Once a policy is mature (for example, once the password policy has been enforced and measured repeatedly), it should be expected to remain at 100 percent compliance.[26] The data used to determine performance against implementation measures is obtained directly from system reports, departmental plans of action, and regular documentation.

Effectiveness and Efficiency Measures

Effectiveness and efficiency measures are one step removed from implementation measures, focusing on whether program-level processes and system-level security controls are implemented according to policy and meet the intended outcomes. These measures focus not only on the effectiveness (robustness, how well it works) of the processes and controls, but also on their efficiency (whether they are implemented in a timely manner). This means that these measures require data based on both the results of processes and the timeline of the process itself to be evaluated.[27]

An example of an effectiveness and efficiency measure is "percentage of network components maintained according to security policy and schedule." Because of the complexity of such metrics, they require both direct data logged by systems and qualitative reports on the implementation of controls. These measures are critical to decision-making within cybersecurity allocations and even policy, as they can reveal misalignments between the prioritization of the effectiveness and efficiency of key aspects of the organization's information systems. For example, if all network components are perfectly maintained according to security policy but not within the specified schedule, breaches and other compromises are still likely despite the investment in effectiveness.

Impact Measures

Finally, impact measures relate directly to the impact of cyber risk management on an organization's operations and bottom line. Typical examples of impact measures include reputation risk mitigated or reputation and trust gained through improved security controls, and direct savings as a result of preventing loss through security improvements.[28]

Consider the measures of all three types that may apply to your organization. How are they reflected in policy? Would you be able to explain who is responsible for reporting on and improving each of these measures? How do these measures align with your organization's concepts of ROI and ROM?

Reviewing Third-Party Agreements

Most organizations have entered into some level of third-party agreement, whether that be with information and communications technology (ICT) service providers such as cloud technology services or with basic operational services such as logistics services.

Before entering into or reviewing any third-party agreements, the organization must first consider the appropriate degree of third-party risk they are willing to expose themselves to. Second, the organization must designate a responsible individual to oversee and guide the management of third-party agreements.

The success of cybersecurity programs depends on willing and capable "owners" for different categories of cyber risk, such as third-party risk.

Legal experts advise that third-party contracts, often referred to as service-level agreements (SLAs), should be developed, monitored, and centralized according to security policies and protocols created with direction from senior management.[29] Key to this process are decisions about what trade-offs are acceptable in relation to the organization's overall risk appetite.

Talent Management

An effective cyber risk management strategy is incomplete without a clear vision for how to build a cyber workforce capable of meeting the evolving challenge of cybersecurity through recruiting and retaining efforts.

The cybersecurity industry has persistently faced a significant skills shortage. While efforts may be made to increase the availability of qualified cybersecurity experts through training, retention is a more nuanced and difficult matter, with job dissatisfaction and underappreciation of cybersecurity skills in the organization being dominant reasons for staff turnover.[30] Staff turnover in cybersecurity teams can be especially damaging to the organization's digital resilience, as the loss of team members is accompanied not only by the loss of their respective skills and expertise, but also by the loss of intimate knowledge of the organization's vulnerabilities and even information asset valuations.

The lack of available cybersecurity professionals and the complexity of cyber risk mean that the need to contract and collaborate with specific functional experts regularly arises when mitigating specific risks. For example, your organization may need to contract compliance experts if mitigating litigation risks. Additionally, in mitigating business operational risks, you may need to contract specific technical experts such as experts in cloud and server application security.

In all these cases, it is essential that management be equipped with the vernacular to communicate confidently with systems and technology and ICT teams as well as third-party functional experts in order to coordinate, oversee, and evaluate their work in any cyber risk mitigation efforts.

Taking Action

Cyber risk management is a responsibility that should be distributed across the entire organization. It is too great a challenge for any one individual. Therefore, establishing a strong cybersecurity culture, entering robust third-party relationships to fill cyber gaps, and sufficiently training the workforce are all critical to the organization's cyber resilience. Here are some concrete actions that can be taken to help distribute cyber responsibilities, whether your organization is larger than Equifax or far smaller.

Building a Cybersecurity Culture

Establishing a culture of security is not completed overnight. Generally, building organizational culture is an exceedingly complex topic that some researchers study over the course of their lifetime. However, there are some simple actions that can be taken to kick-start this process.

One method for fostering a security culture that is both low-cost and fun is through gamifying cybersecurity for the organization. For example, a team at NASA's Jet Propulsion Laboratory created a game called "Donuts." The game is simple: if someone in the group leaves their laptop unlocked, others send an email from the offending laptop to the group's listserv with the subject heading listed as "Donuts." Whoever's laptop was unlocked is then responsible for buying the group donuts on a designated day of the week, and a name-and-shame scoreboard is kept among the group members to keep a tally of who owes everyone donuts.

This was a fun means for energizing the group about cybersecurity. Ultimately, the team stopped playing because everyone consistently locked their computers. While all were disappointed at the lack of donuts because of this, their security culture improved thanks to this little game. Starting a game like this takes little effort and is something that can be done without any infrastructure or considerable planning.

Third-Party Relationships

Almost all organizations will have gaps that need to be filled by third parties. Unfortunately, this increases the surface area of attack for your own organization, as the third-party consultants offer another potential means of entry to attackers. To minimize this risk, there are a couple of simple options available that could help inform your organization of incremental cyber risk associated with engaging with vendors.

One option includes requesting all third parties to have a cyber risk management plan and to share this with your organization. The intention is not to seek a checkbox exercise where vendors may artificially inflate their cyber posture to win your business. Instead, the objective is to see that they have a well-thought-out plan for how to deal with the inevitable cyberattack that impacts them and may have fallout for your own organization.

Another option includes having your third parties' cyber posture objectively evaluated by a cybersecurity rating organization. There are several providers that offer a cyber risk profile of your vendors as a service. While such scorecards may vary in their approach to measuring risk, they can provide a useful snapshot of how seriously your vendors take their own cybersecurity. This should not be the only criterion that a vendor's cyber risk should be evaluated on, but it can be a relatively simple element of your vendor cyber due diligence.

Security Awareness

This chapter's case study emphasizes that people are often the weakest link in a cybersecurity program unless they are trained and educated about threats, vulnerabilities, and how their individual actions can mitigate risk to the organization. In most cases, improving this "human element" of cybersecurity is focused on instilling behavioral change among both individual actors and the organization as a whole. While offering comprehensive security training for employees is anything but a quick process, there are quick wins to be had for raising security awareness.

While some members of the organization may require more specific training and education, awareness training must be pervasive, reaching every level of the organization. Awareness focuses specifically on mitigating cyber risk through addressing the most common risks faced by employees and providing both the skills and processes through which to mitigate these risks—limiting the human vectors for IT and OT security attacks.

Awareness campaigns can be done either online or in person. While major efforts can be undertaken to build awareness—to the point of engaging third parties to help—here we list some of the simpler models that can be implemented quickly and inexpensively (Table 5.1).

Action on the Front Lines

When viewed from the Embedded Endurance perspective, it is easy to see through CEO Richard Smith's efforts to dodge blame. Had Smith pursued cybersecurity with the same fervor he pursued acquisitions, Equifax might not have lost the information of tens of millions of Americans.

Unfortunately, Smith is not the first CEO who failed to embody or build a leadership culture of accountability for cybersecurity. In stark contrast to Smith, however, consider the positive examples of a leader with whom Rosenbach worked closely to make cybersecurity a top priority for the United States military: the former vice chairman of the Joint Chiefs, Admiral James Winnefeld. After a series of successful cyberattacks against the Department of Defense, and the Navy in particular, Admiral Winnefeld led an effort to change the organizational culture in the military to mirror the legendary

Table 5.1 Examples of Simple Awareness Campaigns

Examples of Simple Awareness Campaigns	
Awareness emails or newsletters	Sharing with employees pithy and engaging emails or newsletters that will remind them about the importance of cyber could be both inexpensive and scalable. Something like a cyber fact of the week or interesting news sent to employees that is relevant to their specific role could be a good way to raise awareness. It is important to not overuse this method, though, as it could quickly become ignored by employees.
Ad hoc security testing	Awareness can be raised by engaging employees in security exercises to which they are not necessarily privy. For example, one technique could be sending employees test emails that mimic phishing emails, to check whether the employees are following best practice. Upon their clicking the email (or reporting the email), quick feedback can be delivered that reinforces positive behaviors. This helps to make security a very real and personal experience for employees.
Elevator posters and notices	Something as simple as posting notes in highly trafficked elevators, near entrances or exits, or even in bathrooms that remind employees about good security hygiene (e.g., how to prevent tailgating) can be effective at raising awareness.

leadership of Admiral Hyman Rickover, the "Father of the Nuclear Navy." In more than sixty years, the nuclear-propulsion program that Rickover helped launch did not experience a single accident. Like Rickover, Winnefeld focused intently on the human factor, and sought to formalize cybersecurity reporting metrics from the smallest tactical units up to the headquarters of strategic commands. Additionally, Winnefeld pushed for military leaders to be held accountable for cyber incidents in their organizations, including in their annual performance reviews that are key to promotion within the military ranks.[31]

Main Takeaway

Although the CEO is ultimately accountable for the organization's cybersecurity, managing cyber risk is a major undertaking and too big for any individual to take on. Therefore, it's best to take a systems perspective by distributing responsibility for managing this risk across the organization. The CIO or CISO should not be the only one who holds responsibility. Instead, all business users should know their cyber risk management role and engage in the effort. This may be as direct as becoming a cybersecurity champion, or as simple as taking note of cyber risk awareness campaigns. Without everyone playing a role, there will inevitably be holes in the organization's cyber risk posture.

6

What Risk Prevention Measures Can I Use?

Reducing the likelihood of a successful attack on your organization

Case Study

The Attack

Just as U.S. cybersecurity officials were celebrating their success in protecting the 2020 elections against hackers, authorities uncovered a major cyberattack that had been lurking on critical U.S. systems for the better part of a year.[1] At least nine months prior—as cybersecurity experts were ramping up election defenses—the Russian Foreign Intelligence Service had gained access to the networks of thousands of private and public sector organizations throughout the nation.[2]

How It Happened

Situated at the epicenter of the attack was SolarWinds, a Texas-based IT infrastructure and network management firm with 300,000 customers globally,[3] including more than 80 percent of Fortune 500 companies.[4] The hackers had installed a backdoor in a March 2020 software update that 18,000 SolarWinds customers downloaded, although the intruders exploited their access on a subset of these

Confronting Cyber Risk. Gregory Falco and Eric Rosenbach, Oxford University Press. © Oxford University Press 2022. DOI: 10.1093/oso/9780197526545.003.0006

victims.[5] Accompanying the SolarWinds assault were related attacks involving hits on resellers of Microsoft's cloud computing services and VMware.[6]

The hackers targeted high-value federal entities such as the Department of Homeland Security, the Energy Department (including its National Nuclear Security Administration), and the Treasury Department.[7] Other targets ranged from artificial intelligence chipmaker Nvidia to the California Department of State Hospitals.[8] Especially alarming was the announcement from cybersecurity firm FireEye—the first group to discover the hack—that the infiltrators had stolen a bevy of tools it uses to test its customers' systems for vulnerabilities.[9] FireEye CEO Kevin Mandia summarized, "This attack is different from the tens of thousands of incidents we have responded to throughout the years."[10]

Part of what made this hack so powerful was that it targeted a trusted component of the software supply chain. Orion, the SolarWinds software that was co-opted for the attack, is a network management and monitoring software, and thus organizations regularly grant it pervasive access privileges on their systems.[11] The attackers leveraged these permissions to roam widely on targeted networks. And given the operation's stealth, companies with limited budgets faced a tough choice: conduct a costly (and time-consuming) scrub of their systems or risk the possibility that the attackers maintain a foothold in their networks indefinitely.[12]

Tackling a Major Challenge

Companies and other non-governmental organizations often mistakenly dismiss attacks crafted by foreign governments as "not our problem because we won't be the target." As numerous examples in this book demonstrate, companies routinely occupy the crosshairs of foreign governments and also find themselves among the collateral damage of hits not aimed directly at them. Even a small company may become the "third party" through which a malicious actor tunnels into the networks of bigger organizations—that is, you may be the supply chain attack.

This is one result of the globalized nature of software creation and implementation. In the case described at the start of this chapter, a software company based in the Czech Republic—with research labs in Russia—may have been the means through which Russian agents infiltrated SolarWinds' code.[13] But even this is not new: in 2015 the software firm Netcracker paid over $11 million in fines for having assigned coding work on a U.S. Defense Department project to Russian programmers,[14] a move that may have exposed code and data to Russian intelligence services and allowed them to exploit military networks.[15]

The prospect that attackers can target your organization even through supposedly trusted software suppliers—over which you may have little control—can be daunting. But the SolarWinds attack highlights a crucial lesson: your organization cannot only implement "front door" preventive security measures that attempt to protect the perimeter of your enterprise network. Hackers, whether the Russian intelligence service or less capable cybercriminals, are almost certain to gain access to your internal networks. Every organization must embed measures that allow you to detect, neutralize and recover from any intrusion.

We emphasize throughout this book that cyber risk cannot be fully eliminated, but that organizations can mitigate this risk by leveraging both preventive and resilience measures. Thus the question "What are the prevention measures my organization should utilize?" This chapter provides the most important aspects of preventive risk mitigation measures of Embedded Endurance by focusing on systems, network, data, and physical security.

Why It Matters

Prevention measures require attention to both technological and physical security. While we discuss cybersecurity technologies in the context of systems, networks, and data, it is important to note that these technologies are complementary and overlapping. For example, a technology listed under network protection, such as intrusion detection, plays a very important role in mitigating risk for systems and data connected to the network.

Physical security is often dealt with as a separate department in an organization's overall security strategy. Physical security, however, plays an instrumental role in any organization's efforts to secure systems, networks, and data, and should therefore be integrated with cybersecurity to create an Embedded Endurance approach to securing critical information.

This is a function of the "system of systems" strategy that underlies the Embedded Endurance approach to an organization's digital infrastructure, in which each element of an organization is connected in some way to another. It is critical to think about risk mitigation from the systems perspective because mitigation solutions to a single technology problem fail to effectively address the organization's overall risk.

Key Concepts

1. System security: patches and antivirus
2. Network security: intrusion detection and prevention
3. Data Security: data Governance and Encryption
4. Physical security

Organizations often spend substantial time and money protecting their perimeters to prevent external attackers from gaining access to their systems, networks, and data. This prevention-only approach fails to achieve Embedded Endurance. Many organizations do not focus on protecting their assets against attacks in which either an insider or an outside hacker has already "breached the wire."

System Security: Patches and Antivirus

The software that runs information technology systems is developed by humans. Humans, unfortunately, are fallible and often make mistakes that result in vulnerabilities that attackers seek to exploit using purpose-built malware. More complex software and systems inevitably have more flaws and vulnerabilities, despite dedicated efforts to avoid them in the software development process.

Patch Management

Once software is commercially available, software providers issue patches that repair vulnerabilities in software and firmware that have been identified since the release of the product. Microsoft, for example, issues many patches every month to improve the security of its operating system software.

An effective patch management process is one of the most basic yet most important aspects of preventing cyberattacks against your systems. In short, if Microsoft issues a critical patch for a system in your network, your organization will have an *increased* risk of an intrusion until the patch is applied across the enterprise because attackers know of the vulnerability and systematically scan the internet for organizations that have not applied patches.

Patch management is often overlooked by organizations, either because they see it as an unspoken, commonsense principle that need not be enforced or because they see it as less necessary than software developers may claim. Attackers make good use of these assumptions to launch devastating attacks on individual and networked systems. Still, the SolarWinds case demonstrates how even patches themselves can fall prey to hacks, further emphasizing the need for Embedded Endurance in your organization.

Antivirus

Antivirus (AV) software is a prevention tool that normally runs on individual systems (commonly referred to as endpoints) connected to a network, such as a laptop or mobile device. This software scans files to match patterns of known malware and viruses called malware signatures. The most effective AV software will also utilize heuristics and artificial intelligence to detect hackers' attempts to exploit known vulnerabilities in unpatched software applications. Such heuristics could even include behavioral monitoring to help detect unusual activity. It is worth noting that most antivirus tools require a considerable amount of memory and processing power to run, making them less viable for use on IoT devices, which are resource-constrained. Thus, other types of endpoint protection techniques are necessary, such as the use of process whitelisting, which restricts what types of processes are allowed to run on the system.

Network Security: Intrusion Detection and Prevention

Historically, organizations devoted the majority of preventive cybersecurity efforts to keeping hackers outside of their trusted networks. Over the past several years, security experts have realized that they must not only protect the perimeter of their networks, but also deploy technologies that will allow them to detect malicious activity on their internal, trusted networks. The SolarWinds case illustrates the importance of effective intrusion detection and intrusion prevention systems because the Russian attackers' use of SolarWinds would never have been caught without technology that identified anomalous behavior on the victims' networks. Intrusion detection and prevention systems (collectively referred to as IDPSs) generally take the form of software or applications that scan the flow of data on a network for malicious behavior. Intrusion detection systems (IDSs) and intrusion prevention systems (IPSs) can, depending on their configuration:

- Report intrusions or attempted intrusions to the network
- Take actions to prevent intrusions
- Decrease the impact of intrusions on the network

While they are generally integrated into one IDPS product, there are subtle—but important—differences between the two types of intrusion systems.[16] These are outlined in Table 6.1.

Table 6.1 IDS vs. IPS

IDS vs. IPS	
Intrusion detection system	These are devices that passively monitor network traffic and run processes to identify potential threats. An IDS is designed to scan and analyze data packets to detect anomalous activity that could be a security breach. When signs of unauthorized access are detected, the IDS generates a log message that provides detailed information about the breach, such as when it occurred and what actions were taken. Depending on configurations, the log may immediately be escalated for the attention of relevant security team members.[*]
Intrusion prevention system	Similar to IDSs, IPSs are devices or applications designed to monitor data packets for unauthorized access. However, where IPSs differ from IDSs is that when a packet is identified as malicious, the packet is rejected and does not pass through the perimeter network into the internal network.[**] If so configured, the system may also stop the attack by terminating the network connection or reconfiguring the firewalls, routers, and switches in the system to block access to the targeted system (for example, a mail server) completely. An IPS can also neutralize an attack's content (for example, remove an infected attachment from an email).

* Bradley, T. 2017. "Introduction to Intrusion Detection Systems (IDS)." LifeWire. https://www.lifewire.com/introduction-to-intrusion-detection-systems-ids-2486799.

** Palo Alto Networks. 2017. "What Is an Intrusion Prevention System?" https://www.paloaltonetworks.com/cyberpedia/what-is-an-intrusion-prevention-system-ips.

IDPSs are primarily classified as either host-based intrusion detection systems (HIDS) (most relevant to systems) or network-based intrusion detection systems (NIDS) (most relevant to networks). That said, an important trend in cybersecurity is to move to cloud-based intrusion detection capabilities that allow the organization to outsource the complicated and resource-intensive work of operating and monitoring these technologies.

It is important to identify a threat in its early stages, as the attackers might not have gained access to any important data or systems (for example, an infrastructure breach has occurred, but no data breach has taken place yet). This means IDPS systems should be monitored on an ongoing basis. Early detection will minimize "dwell time," which is the period between when the system was compromised and when the threat is contained.[17] Early detection can help to prevent lateral movement, which is when an attacker moves from one system or department to another within an organization with the aim of causing as much damage as possible.[18]

Precursors and Indicators

Although cyberattacks are usually only detected once the attacker has gained access to the system, there are some precursors (warnings or signs) to look out for that could indicate that an attack may take place in the future. These include the following:

- Logs showing that a vulnerability scanner has been used without the incident response or IT team's knowledge. A vulnerability scanner is a program that detects the weak points within systems and networks. It can be used internally to identify areas the organization should address. However, if an external party gains access to the system and runs the scanner, it can reveal further weaknesses that can be exploited.
- A new threat that has been identified by the broader IT community, which targets elements in systems that the organization knows are currently vulnerable or weak.
- A direct threat that is made against the organization (such as in the case of a ransomware attack).[19]

Once a precursor has been detected, the organization can make use of the opportunity to strengthen its security processes and monitor the threat closely.

Indicators are signs that an attack is under way or has already happened. There are many different examples of indicators, including the following:

- Systems acting sluggishly or in unusual ways
- Unusually heavy network traffic
- Many bounced emails
- Deactivation of antivirus software
- The creation of new user accounts
- Log files that have been cleaned out

- Unsuccessful attempts to log in from unfamiliar systems[20]

As a myriad of indicators might show that an attack is under way, detection tools should be used to keep track of these. The "Taking Action" section explains tools that your organization can use to spot hacks.

Data Security: Data Governance and Encryption

It's now conventional wisdom that "data is the new oil." Though this statement is likely hyperbole, every organization must focus on protecting sensitive and important data. The most effective preventive measures for protecting data are data governance programs, encryption, and data loss prevention technologies.

Data Governance
The rules and processes an organization establishes in the handling, sharing, and accessing of its data have a direct impact on operational risk, reputational risk, and litigation risk. In many cases, how an organization processes its data is based on laws and regulations that govern data usage in the organization's sector.

Encryption
Cryptography is the practice of using codes to store information in such a way that it is accessible only to those for whom the information is intended. In theory, cryptographic tools can provide near-perfect data privacy, but as with most systems, their effectiveness can be undermined by human error and mismanagement. Cryptographic techniques are usually complemented with encryption, which transforms otherwise intelligible data or text, known as plaintext, by applying a mathematical algorithm that makes the data unintelligible. The encrypted data can be decrypted only with a key given to authorized individuals by the originator of the data.

Data Loss Prevention Technology

Similar to the technology used for intrusion detection systems, data loss prevention tools provide organizations with the ability to detect when critical data has been exfiltrated from secure locations.

Before investigating the methods used to protect data, it's important to understand the three states that data can have within an organization (Table 6.2): at rest, in use, and in motion.[21]

Physical Security

Physical security prevents unauthorized physical access that may compromise cybersecurity or the technology required for the continued functioning of information systems.[22]

At its foundation, information security is concerned with maintaining the confidentiality, integrity, and availability of the information systems that organizations depend on to meet their business objectives. Physical security aims to protect the physical assets that support an organization's information systems by fulfilling two essential requirements, both of which are focused on prevention.

The first requirement is that physical security prevents damage to or theft of the infrastructure that supports the organization's digital systems. The second requirement for physical security is to prevent intentional or negligent misuse of the infrastructure that may

Table 6.2 Data States

Data States	
At rest	When data is stored on a relatively stationary and permanent device such as a computer or server, it is referred to as data at rest.
In use	This refers to any data that is being actively accessed, for example, someone opening a project timing spreadsheet.
In motion	Data that is being shared or moved around. For example, data being sent via email or shared via a USB drive or portable hard drive is considered to be in motion. Data being shared over direct networks is also classified as "in transit."

potentially expose the information system to harm. This may include unauthorized access to the infrastructure, vandalism, or the theft of components, to name a few.[23]

Physical security relies on numerous different types of devices for preventing and detecting unauthorized access. Physical barriers, such as sophisticated locks and doors, prevent access to information system technologies, while detection devices, such as alarms and sensors, alert security teams in the event of a security breach.

While cybersecurity may prevent hackers from accessing information systems online, once hackers have physical access to a device connected to an organization's network, they can generally leverage that physical access to advance their hacking efforts. In many cases, all hackers require to hack a system is the ability to physically plug a memory device into an accessible terminal. This would allow them to install any range of malware and, potentially, move laterally throughout the organization's networks (provided those networks have not been sufficiently protected).

Going Deeper

System Protection

Host-Based IDSs

HIDSs reside on a single computer or device and monitor that specific device for changes. Host-based IDPSs protect servers and host information assets. A host-based IDPS will run directly on the device it protects (for example, a mail server).

HIDSs can be used on mission-critical systems such as servers where needed configuration changes are rare. Often, a unique cryptographic hash (an encryption technique that renders the output unrecognizable from the input while it travels through the network) is created for the files on that system. Any subsequent change to those files will then cause a different hash (a new encrypted version) to be created when checking the integrity of the files. This will trigger the HIDS to notify network administrators that an intruder is attempting to access the file assets.[24]

Host-based IDPSs can only monitor, analyze, and control traffic that originates or is received by the specific host. Any suspicious activity elsewhere in the network will not be detected by a host-based IDPS. If the host is compromised by the attack, the IDPS is more likely to be compromised with it (disabled, for example). However, as they do not require the purchase of additional hardware, they are a cost-effective option for small networks with few hosts. Their other major benefit is that they can monitor all users' activities that involve the host device, which is not possible with a network-based system.

Antivirus

Antivirus software can also be classified as a type of HIDS since it works directly on the host device. This software scans files to match patterns of known malware and viruses called malware signatures. If configured to do so, the software may also employ control of certain critical directories to prevent installation of malware in the first place, making it more of an integrated intrusion detection and prevention system.

Some antivirus platforms also use heuristics (tests based on up-to-date information about behaviors, existing and previous threats) to identify previously unknown threats. These software packages may also automatically send data from the host computer to the vendor to identify new threats and add them to the known threat database.

Antivirus software generally makes use of three prominent types of heuristic detection methods:

1. **Sandbox testing:** Also known as file emulation, sandbox testing observes the file's behavior in a controlled setting. If the file displays the characteristics of a virus, the file is labeled as a virus and dealt with accordingly by the antivirus software.
2. **File analysis:** This type of detection analyzes the file to determine the file's destination and its intent once that destination has been reached.

3. **Genetic signature detection:** Although viruses vary in the functions they perform, many share similar characteristics, as they often tend to be modified from existing viruses. Genetic detection uses known virus definitions to identify malicious files that may be disguised as trusted or safe files.

Network Protection

Network-Based IDSs

Network-based IDPSs and NIDSs are not installed on hosts themselves. Instead, they operate on separate devices called sensors, placed at strategic locations within the network. They monitor network traffic and identify or act upon packets that may present a threat. These systems monitor all data passing through a specific point in the network, which can involve several devices.[25] They compare network traffic to known threat signatures and other traffic on the same network to identify anomalous occurrences. This approach, called anomaly detection, is based on the statistical likelihood of a packet being legitimate. For example, if 98 percent of legitimate traffic looks a certain way, but a new packet looks significantly different, it is probable that the differing packet should not be moving through that network.

As NIDSs and network-based IDPSs do not operate on the hosts themselves, these systems are less likely to be compromised along with the host device. However, since network-based monitors check all incoming and outgoing traffic at a network "intersection," they must be carefully configured for fast, reliable performance. Otherwise, they can become a bottleneck, slowing down traffic as they analyze all packets. An overloaded NIDS can experience errors, sever network connections, or shut down temporarily (leaving the system more open to intrusion), and can therefore be as bad as having no IDS at all. This is a major potential pain point for organizations running 24/7 systems and why some of them do not use NIDSs or network-based IDPSs.

Firewalls

A firewall is a network device or software application that analyzes packet headers and rejects, accepts, or flags them based on its configurations and security policy. Firewalls can be configured by including or excluding different filters that dictate what types of data, sources, or entities can access a system. Based on their configuration, firewalls reject packets that do not comply with protocol types, source or destination addresses, or source or destination ports that have been predefined as acceptable. For example, Simple Mail Transfer Protocol (SMTP) is a protocol used to send and receive emails over the internet. Firewalls can be configured to accept or reject emails depending on whether or not they meet the SMTP permissions set out in the firewall configuration.

Firewalls assist in creating a perimeter around the organization's internal networks to protect them from untrusted connections, unauthorized access requests, and malicious data. The network protected by the perimeter can therefore be deemed "trusted." Firewalls need not only serve as "front door" security; organizations can use them within networks to mitigate the access of hackers who have made it into one part of the system.

Given the similarity between NIDS and firewalls (both analyze and reject anomalous packets), these products have converged over time.

Security Policies

Trust is a concept that regularly comes up in discussing network protection; it is taken to mean that a device or network will reliably enforce the specified security policy.[26] An untrusted device, connection, or system is therefore one in which the security policy cannot be enforced. For example, the firewall can be configured to enforce the organization's security policy, but the connection to the internet provided by the internet service provider (ISP) cannot.

When accessing the internet, it is important that the web pages people access originate from trusted sources, to prevent users from accessing dummy sites that may facilitate cyberattacks. Certificate authorities issue digital certificates that verify whether the identities of digital entities are trustworthy. Internet browsers and operating systems maintain an updated list of trusted root certificates issued to entities to protect users from exposure to harmful entities.[27] A digital certificate generally contains information such as the owner's name and the public key, which is used to encrypt data and verify the legitimacy of the owner's digital signature. However, as seen in past attacks, certificate authorities are not always entirely trustworthy.

Data Protection

Encryption

Organizations cannot decide on effective encryption approaches without understanding and categorizing the state of the data they possess. For example, if an organization stores a significant amount of data on portable hard drives, it would be irresponsible not to enforce hard drive encryption. Similarly, if sensitive data is frequently shared via digital means, such as email, file encryption or the use of virtual private networks should be prioritized. It is important to keep in mind that, given the changing nature of data in the current cyber landscape, the lines that separate the three states of data are not always clearly defined.

The choice of software- or hardware-based encryption depends heavily on the state of the data the organization aims to protect. Depending on the state of the data, best practice advises the following:[28]

1. **Data at rest:** Should your data be in this state, opt for hardware-based encryption that protects all data on the hard disk of the device the data is stored on—from file directories to the actual file contents themselves. Encryption of data at rest prevents data breaches when an attacker gains physical access to the machine. When using such a solution, ensure that the device demands user authentication before booting up (starting) so that the operating system will not run if the user is not authorized to access data on the device. In this case, encryption

should have minimal effect on system performance while adding considerable security. With laptop encryption, for example, even though the laptop might fall into the wrong hands, only the owner of the laptop will be able to decrypt the data that is stored on the laptop's hard drive.

2. **Data in use:** You typically need to decrypt any active data to work with it, which creates a significant gap in data security. If data is being simultaneously uploaded to the cloud as it is being worked on, the efficiency and quality of cloud encryption becomes paramount and is not always ensured with free-to-use or less expensive software-as-a-service (SaaS) suites. Current best practice dictates protecting data in use with software solutions (file encryption) as well as stringent access control. The encryption of data in use is an ongoing problem. One possible solution may be homomorphic encryption, which is a way of performing calculations on encrypted data without the need to first decrypt the data; however, this is still largely in the proof-of-concept stage and is not available for public use. Therefore, it is important to engage with cloud providers who encrypt data quickly as real-time updates are made.

3. **Data in motion:** Sensitive information is especially vulnerable in motion, particularly when being transferred outside trusted networks of your organization, because attackers will try to intercept, copy, or steal it. To protect data in motion, your organization should try to use file-level encryption transferred over a virtual private network (VPN). With file-level encryption, each file should be individually encrypted and remain encrypted until unlocked by the intended recipient. VPN technology creates an encrypted "tunnel" between two trusted systems, thus thwarting attempts to steal or manipulate sensitive data in motion.

Encryption is often viewed as a silver bullet for confidentiality and integrity as, in theory, it should render data unrecognizable unless decoded by an authorized user and device. However, a single encryption solution is rarely enough to fully support confidentiality and security at large. Instead, consider a layered approach, also referred to as "defense in depth," that creates several barriers to entry for attackers. Future concerns with encryption include how quantum computers may be able to break current encryption methods, rendering its protection ineffective.

Converging Physical Security and Cybersecurity

With the growth of the Internet of Things, the number of physical devices connected to the internet is rapidly increasing, as is the number of OT systems, both of which have implications in the physical world. As a result, there is an increasing interest in integrating physical and cybersecurity functions to mitigate cyber threats to digital systems. Most organizations have separate departments that deal exclusively with physical security and cybersecurity, respectively. Failure to converge these two forms of security may hamper an organization's cybersecurity efforts.

Securing information systems requires coordinating cybersecurity and physical security efforts. Cyberattacks could undermine physical security measures, while physical attacks allow unauthorized access to crucial cyber assets. As a result, the goal of an organization is thus to integrate both types of security in their defense.

The convergence of physical security and cybersecurity should be applied over three areas: personnel, facilities, and data.[29]

Personnel
Identity management is key to information security. By monitoring users' identities, security teams can implement processes that apply roles and responsibilities to each user's identity. This responsibility may fall on the cybersecurity team, but identity management may also be combined with a building's security controls to limit physical access to rooms that house important information system technology.

Identity management is the administrative task of identifying individuals who are authorized to access an information system, and allocating access permissions based on each person's identity.

An organization's physical security team can contribute to identity management by regulating access to the technologies connected to information systems. This can be combined with the cybersecurity team's capacity to monitor those same users and keep track of the computers they use, the servers they access, and their level of authorization within networks and databases. If identity management is left to separate physical and cybersecurity systems, it increases the likelihood that the two systems may become unsynchronized, creating a vulnerable gap in information security.

Combining physical and cybersecurity systems allows for accuracy in the management of identity data, ensuring that access is effectively regulated despite changes to personnel. In many cases, for example, if employment is terminated, employees are escorted off the organization's premises to prevent appropriation of trade secrets or compromise of data integrity. However, if the termination is not registered with the team responsible for information security soon enough, employees may still use their remote access to the company's networks to cause harm to the networks.

Facilities

Securing an organization's facilities is typically considered the responsibility of the physical security team. However, with many organizations allowing employees access to information systems through wireless networks, physical facilities now also extend into "virtual" facilities. Employees are thus no longer required to be in the physical location of the organization to access its networks. With access no longer limited to the physical confines of the organization, security teams need to ensure that those who are not permitted to access networks are restricted from doing so.

Physical Data Protection

Physical security and cybersecurity may be combined to protect data in two ways. First, organizations can ensure the safety of the assets that employees use to access critical data, such as laptops, mobile phones, and tablets. The physical security team should ensure that all assets that could potentially be used to access the organization's information systems are housed in secure locations. The information security team, on the other hand, should secure the same assets with safeguards (such as disk encryption, password protection, or antivirus software) that protect the data stored on those devices, and should ensure that only authorized users can access the operating systems on those devices.

The second way to protect data is to restrict access to the hardware that stores critical data, such as hard drives and servers. Although organizations are increasingly making use of cloud storage service providers, many rely on storing their data on servers housed in specific rooms or even warehouses. In cases such as this, physical security and cybersecurity may again converge to create a robust security strategy. Prior to gaining physical access to the technology that stores critical data, employees should first be required to provide identification that they are in fact authorized to access the technology. This could be in the form of a physical key fob or ID card that needs to be presented for access. Data security can then be bolstered by applying cybersecurity on top of physical security—for example, via an application of password protection to the technology that is required to access the data.

Taking Action

Preventive risk mitigation can be achieved by employing tools and processes; however, it is important to remember that these come at a cost. Limited organizational resources require prioritized action on systems, networks, and data. Given this reality, we propose some basic steps an organization can take that require minimal financial investment and serve as a starting point for enabling both risk prevention and resilience.

Patch Management

Software patches are rolled out to address security flaws, but if software is not kept up to date, these flaws remain open and vulnerable. Table 6.3 includes a process that can be adopted for patch management, as recommended by the SANS Institute.[30]

Table 6.3 A Process for Patch Management

A Process for Patch Management	
Assessment and indexing	Regularly update an inventory of all servers, routers, printers, and networked devices. This inventory should include an assessment of the operating system, key applications, and firmware of each device, and also reflect how a change to one device could affect overall operations.
Testing	Create a test environment that mimics the operational environment as closely as possible; for example, build a microcosm of your company intranet. It should represent each device that the inventory determined as mission-critical. Use this "sandbox" to determine whether a new software or firmware patch may impact operations, or even result in a loss of data or access to key systems.
Backup	Before any patch is deployed, systems should be in place that back up server and device information. This is critical in case systems need to be restored to their previous state if unforeseen problems occur during or after patching.
Patch evaluation	Determine critical patch criteria and preferable patch schedules. While ideally every system should be patched with the most frequent versions, this is not always practical. Management and functional experts need to work together to determine which patches are most critical. Many major operating systems and software packages can be configured to update automatically.
Review and notification	System owners and functional managers should review the potential impact of patching and decide whether or when to implement it. Any personnel who may be affected should be notified when patching will be implemented and told how to report adverse effects.
Patch rollout	Implement patching in off-peak times, if possible, to mitigate operational risk. If a patch is an emergency fix, this may not be possible. Make every effort to limit disruptions to workflow and access to information assets.
Maintenance	Designate patch management teams and roles as well as responsibility for updating relevant policies and procedures. As with any high-risk project, a project owner needs to be identified and report to executive management on changes, concerns, and progress. Documentation is essential to mitigating risk and should be reviewed regularly to address evolving threat vectors and actors.

Protecting Data

Data Governance

Without effective data governance, data quality is uncontrolled and can be compromised. Data governance provides an organizing framework for establishing strategy, policy, and objectives for managing data that the organization generates and collects. It also assigns rights to and accountability for data-related processes.

The state of an enterprise's data governance and the quality of its ongoing cyber risk management can greatly affect the organization's desirability in an acquisition or merger. This is because organizations entering into an ownership or partnership agreement can become liable for the litigation risks of the organizations they acquire or merge with.

Data Governance Team

To derive business value from data governance, specific, appropriate individuals should be assigned to the organization's data governance team (DGT).

While policies and principles should be outlined in the creation of the enterprise security policy (ESP) in collaboration with senior management and functional professionals, the data governance team (DGT) becomes responsible for translating relevant policies into business requirements and guidelines, and helps to enforce them from a business perspective. In other words, the DGT enhances ongoing management efforts by closing the gap between data governance policy creation and enforcement. Additionally, DGTs communicate the business value of data governance policies to relevant stakeholders and become responsible for ensuring that those stakeholders have a sufficient understanding of the risks and consequences when data architecture and management guidelines are ignored.[31]

Finally, the DGT is expected to collaborate with leadership to determine the extent to which the business expectations on data governance and data security are realistic given current resources and other considerations.

The DGT should include some IT staff and representatives from every major department within the organization to ensure pervasive adherence to policy and comprehensive feedback to leadership.

Data Stewards

To further improve accountability and accuracy both in the management of data and in how data concerns are communicated within the organization, it is advisable to appoint data stewards. Data stewardship refers to the management of an organization's data assets so that users have easy access to necessary data. The number of stewards depends on the size of the organization, the amount of data it needs to manage as set out in the ESP.

In many organizations, data stewardship commonly defaults to a de facto role—for example, to managers or information and communications technology (ICT) team members. Most data stewardship programs have limited long-term viability, as they often lack well-defined, measurable goals with specific expectations and vision for what data stewardship means for the organization's risk management. Data stewardship thus requires appropriate budget allocation as well as consistent oversight and accountability.

In growing or complex organizations, it is often simplest to assign a data steward to a specific business process. This person is then responsible for the data domains, applications, and systems that form part of a particular process. In the case of larger or more mission-critical processes, multiple stewards may be assigned.[32] In certain cases, a full-time data steward may even be assigned to a process. This model is often successful because it can combine function- or domain-specific knowledge—such as information from managers—with technical and data governance expertise like that from the chief information security officer.

Data Architecture

Data architecture is a framework that outlines what data exists in which location and how it is moved through the organization's networks. Should the business require different data practices or need to adjust its systems according to new regulation or due to vulnerabilities, the DGT is able to analyze these issues using the data architecture and appropriate metrics.

The details of data architecture documentation should focus on the changes that data may undergo as it moves from one network or system to the next. These resources are invaluable to the DGT and data stewards in both communicating concerns regarding data management and in making effective decisions regarding data policy in the organization. These resources are also important in determining where useful business data (business intelligence) may be extracted from the organization's systems. Finally, inventory and flow diagrams can help stakeholders predict potential vulnerabilities and weak points across a network that may expose the organization to increased cyber risk.[33]

Master Data Management

Master data management (MDM), in short, involves managing data about data—in other words, managing the context around how the data is stored, used, and moved around in the organization.[34] For example, the organization may be handling a particular piece of customer information, such as the details of a purchase to be shipped from the warehouse, but the context around this transaction also needs to be processed and managed. This context appears as data in different points of the business process, including personally identifiable information (PII) like the customer's address, the payment information, the adjusted inventory system of the affected warehouse, and so on. All of this contextual information is affected by MDM.

As master data is generally required for processing transactions, organizing reporting structures, and business process analysis, the types of data covered by MDM include:[35]

- Data about internal organizational entities, such as employees, products sold, and departments
- Data concerning external entities, such as suppliers and customers
- Data that relates to the chart of accounts and the organization's hierarchical reporting structure

MDM often denotes reference data in particular, such as rosters of employees or vendors, or updated inventories.

MDM policy is frequently investigated in the case of mergers and acquisitions, in ensuring regulatory compliance, and in auditing to track, for example, the routing (movement) of documents and funds.

Data Minimization

Data minimization dictates that any data that is collected and processed should be stored (retained) only for as long as necessary. This concept has become an essential principle of data protection. Many organizations have vast quantities of data stored, hoping to extract business intelligence from the information later. However, the trend toward storing data that is not in active use for potential future benefit has introduced prime opportunities for malicious actors to access or compromise data.

Preparing Your Cyber Defense Tools

Cyberattacks can be detected either using automated tools or manually by individuals who become aware of problems (such as employees and customers who report that they have trouble accessing the organization's systems or website).

Tools You Can Use to Detect and Prevent Cyberattacks

Visibility across all the organization's networks and systems is necessary to detect threats. However, the size of many organizations makes it almost impossible to keep track of networks and systems manually. Automated threat detection tools are therefore becoming increasingly important, ensuring that the response team has the information it needs to act on threats.[36] These tools should show system analysts what is happening across the organization, and should flag abnormal activity, such as unusual amounts of traffic on a network. To identify abnormal activity, the criteria for normal activity should be established first.

It is also important that your organization filter and contextualize the data obtained through an automated system (for example, only data that meets certain criteria is shown, and normal activity is contrasted with the observed activity). This will provide the response team with a clear visual overview of the situation, which may reduce reaction time and improve decision-making.[37]

In addition to those already discussed, some of the automated tools you can use to detect cyberattacks—whether by identifying precursors or indicators—are listed in Table 6.4.

It is important to remember that human analysis of data obtained from detection tools is necessary, as machines are not always capable of understanding the context of the data obtained. Your organization may choose to appoint security analysts or establish security operations centers (SOCs) that are dedicated to monitoring all data obtained from automated detection tools and responding accordingly. Smaller organizations may not have the resources available to establish an SOC, increasing the importance of having a clear communication plan in place and practicing for events. There are, however, some outsourced SOC services available in the market that are customized to the needs of small and medium-sized enterprises.[38]

Action on the Front Lines

In a world of complex software and hardware supply chains, you can never fully expect that your organization's IT and OT are risk-free. This sharpens the importance of leveraging leadership to embed endurance throughout the organization. Certainly those entities impacted by the SolarWinds attack would have been better off adopting preventative tools to monitor and address threats from even trusted suppliers.

Given the range of threats that pose risks at your organization's cyber "front door," it is often easy to ignore risks elsewhere, or at least accept them as an unfortunate and unalterable reality. This was absolutely the case for Falco's clients as he ran his industrial Internet of Things security company that worked with global energy utility

Table 6.4 Automated Security Tools

Tool	Description
Intrusion detection and prevention system (IDPS) logs	When the IDPS detects a known event, it generates a detailed log message providing information about the event. Depending on configurations, the log may immediately be escalated for the attention of relevant security team members.
System and application logs	Logs record all the actions performed on a system or application. If an organization knows what its activity normally looks like, alerts can be generated if unusual activity is noted.
Security information and event management (SIEM) products	These work in a similar fashion to an IDPS, but analyze logs and issue alerts based on the data contained within activity logs.
File integrity checking software	This software identifies changes made to computer files, by calculating checksums and comparing them to previous checksums. (A checksum is derived by an algorithm that calculates a unique number for a set of data. If a component within the data is changed, the checksum also changes. Comparing the original checksum with the current checksum therefore verifies data integrity.)
Anti-spam software	This type of software detects spam messages and stops them from being delivered to mailboxes. Although receiving spam is not always an indication of a cyberattack, these messages may contain content that could lead to an attack.
Firewall logs	Logs generated by firewalls may be used to correlate alerts generated by other devices.
Network analyzers	These are used to detect any unusual network traffic, which may be an indication of a cyberattack.
Availability monitoring	One of the first signs that an incident has occurred is often the fact that users are having trouble accessing servers or applications. This tool will assist in identifying these problems, which can then be followed up to determine whether it relates to a cyberattack.
Vulnerability scanners	These can be run to identify any vulnerabilities within the system that can be corrected.

providers. While OT organizations often first aim to secure their networks or their data, they have the least security control over their endpoints. This is especially true of their control systems, such as assets like the software-defined motor of a wind turbine or a smart meter. The CIO of a multinational renewable energy conglomerate Falco worked with was well informed about cyber risks and had an incredibly progressive network and data security agenda; however, the endpoints of the electric grid were always a delicate topic. "The OEM controls those," the CIO said, and continued, "They [the OEM] will void our warranty if we try to install anything on those devices that are not authorized." Given the delicate dynamic between the parties, Falco and the utility CIO then tried meeting with the chief technology officer (CTO) of their smart meter provider. Over the phone, the CTO insisted that their smart meter was secure and there was no reason to enhance its security; even as he was saying that, Falco and his team demonstrated in real time a gaping vulnerability in their system using publicly available information. This only ended up further irritating the CTO of the smart meter company, who threatened repercussions for the demonstration and quickly hung up the phone. Ultimately, the CIO of the utility had to work with his chief procurement officer and legal team to embed language in future procurement contracts requiring OEMs to allow security modifications to their devices without voiding the warranty.

This example demonstrates that across a supply chain there are many layers of security interventions possible and a variety of stakeholders that control them. Even if a technical solution or set of protection tools to reduce risk is feasible, there are social, political, contractual, and other legal variables across the supply chain of your operations and digital infrastructure that could lead to implementation challenges. As the case of Falco's utility client demonstrates, provisioning for protections in contracting is one means for embedding security in your organization's supply chain beyond installing protective tools.

Main Takeaway

Cyber risk is a function of the threat that attackers pose to the vulnerabilities of important systems, data, and networks. Organizations will never completely eliminate risk, but measures that attempt to prevent hackers from achieving malicious success can mitigate risk. Most cybersecurity efforts focus primarily on technical mitigation measures; however, the Embedded Endurance strategy emphasizes that effective implementation of patch management and data governance processes are crucial to decreasing an organization's overall cyber risk profile.

7

What Risk Resilience Measures Can I Use?

Reducing the impact and consequences of successful cyberattacks

Case Study

"While I am grateful that the perpetrator has been caught, I am deeply sorry for what has happened. I sincerely apologize for the understandable worry this incident must be causing those affected and I am committed to making it right."[1] Seemingly overnight, Capital One chairman and CEO Richard Fairbank had found himself facing one of the largest digital breaches in banking history.[2]

What Happened?

In July 2019 Fairbank learned of a staggering breach that had allowed a hacker months of unauthorized access to over 100 million customers' personal data. This included 140,000 social security numbers, 80,000 bank account details, and information from credit card applications spanning more than a decade. The company estimated the breach's price tag at up to $150 million in 2019 alone.[3]

At the hack's root was Paige Thompson, a former Amazon Web Services employee. Thompson had found a misconfigured firewall in Capital One's system, and in March 2019 accessed the company's

Confronting Cyber Risk. Gregory Falco and Eric Rosenbach, Oxford University Press. © Oxford University Press 2022. DOI: 10.1093/oso/9780197526545.003.0007

consumer data.[4] "Dude, so many people are doing it wrong," wrote Thompson in an online message describing how many companies had made the same mistake.[5] She would later be indicted for breaching more than thirty organizations.[6]

The Response

Fairbank knew this was a crucial moment, one for which he had been preparing. Relative to other large banks, Capital One was an early adopter of cloud services, migrating the personal data of its customers onto AWS servers beginning around 2014.[7] Speaking with shareholders months before his company discovered the breach, Fairbank described his firm as "one of the most cloud-forward companies in the world."[8]

Alert to the cyber risks involved, the CEO and his top executives reportedly had scrutinized other major companies' responses to cybersecurity disasters, conducting their own analyses of where firms had failed and why.[9]

Therefore, Fairbank took a hands-on approach in the immediate aftermath of Capital One's breach, even carefully writing and editing personal apologies to customers and employees. The day Capital One disclosed the hack, Fairbank wrote to his organization, "This is a defining moment for us to put our values on display and to be swift, open, and profoundly empathetic."[10]

Learning to Do Better

Most obviously, his cybersecurity unit had failed to prevent and detect the breach. Months passed before an email from an outside source alerted it to the catastrophe—the tipster had come across reams of Capital One's customer data online.[11] Yet even prior to the incident the company's cyber team was a concern. High attrition rates roiled the group's senior ranks, and a third of its employees departed in the year before the attack.[12] When the cybersecurity unit finally did detect the intrusion, the damage was already well advanced.

Meanwhile, the bank's response irked customers and government officials alike. Two months after Capital One discovered the breach, members of the U.S. Senate Committee on Banking, Housing and Urban Affairs wrote to Fairbank, "To date, we believe Capital One has not taken sufficient steps to make good on its commitment to protect consumers from further harm."[13] The senators especially criticized the bank's processes for providing credit monitoring and identity protection to customers.[14]

One week after news of the incident broke, the bank's stock had plummeted 11 percent.[15] Outside the firm, the breach was ammunition for those wary of migrating data to the cloud. Cybersecurity professionals noted that hundreds of Amazon accounts had been found vulnerable to a similar issue just a month before Thompson gained access to Capital One's servers; when the situation was viewed this way, it was possible to see the bank as having simply drawn the short straw. And the concerns multiplied for those in heavily regulated industries like banking and healthcare.

In this chapter, we'll address the question that Fairbank faced on a July morning in 2019: *What do I do when my organization has been hacked?* This chapter discusses the various measures you should take to plan for and react to a cyberattack so that your organization can be resilient to such attacks.

Why It Matters

Despite your best efforts to prevent a cyberattack, your organization will almost certainly suffer a hack at some point over the next several years. Thus, when you get hit, you need the ability to bounce back and resume normal operations. Resilience is the ability to recover quickly from impacts and is foundational to the Embedded Endurance strategy of mitigating cyber risk. A resilient organization mitigates risk by reducing the overall consequences of the attack on the mission, operations, and overall costs.

For example, an organization that employs technical resilience measures, such as virtualizing important operational platforms and leveraging a cloud-based solution for readily available backups, will be able to resume operations relatively quickly. Resuming operations lowers the potential mission impact of the attack, but to address all of the risks related to financial losses, litigation, and reputational damage an organization must also have a formal incident response and crisis communications plan

This chapter focuses on bolstering an organization's resilience in three ways: deploying important technologies, implementing a formal incident response plan, and crafting a cyber crisis communication plan.

Key Concepts

1. Technical resilience measures
2. Cyber incident response: building a plan and a team
3. Cyber crisis communication plan

Technical Resilience Measures

Virtualization

Cloud services are omnipresent in today's modern computing world. They offer organizations the opportunity to perform necessary computing operations without having to manage the associated computing infrastructure. There are often direct security benefits to engaging cloud service providers—especially for smaller organizations that do not have the security resources to manage and maintain a robust security program.

An additional benefit is the digital resilience that virtualizing computing processes enable. Cloud service providers generally commit to extremely high uptime guarantees in their service-level agreements. They are able to do this by hosting your organization's applications and content on a series of parallel-running servers located in different locations. This affords organizations the ability to maintain uptime even if a given service area experiences an outage or security incident.

Backups

Backup technologies are a critical aspect of organizational resilience. In short, backup technologies make a copy of the data or software configuration used by the organization and store it in a secure location, including the cloud, that is inaccessible to hackers. During a cyberattack (or other crisis-like scenarios, like a hurricane) an organization's key data and systems may become unavailable. For example, an organization hit by a ransomware attack often loses access to important data and operational platforms. Ideally, the organization procured and deployed backup technologies that would allow it to access the backup data or configuration, operationalize it, and bounce back to normal operations.

Cyber Incident Response: Building a Plan and a Team

You don't want to start thinking about how to react to a cyber-attack *after* the cyberattack has occurred. Incident response planning should begin well before a hack occurs. The incident response process should be both proactive and reactive. Table 7.1 outlines recommended steps to follow during an incident response process.

Prevention, planning, and preparation are proactive steps that are taken prior to an attack. The other steps in the process are reactive, and focus on what the organization should do to manage the consequences of an attack once it has occurred. Note that steps 4–8 are iterative, and lessons learned in the post-event analysis should feed back into planning for the next incident response.

Table 7.1 The Incident Response Process

The Incident Response Process	
	1. Prevention
Proactive	2. Planning
	3. Preparation
	4. Detection
	5. Analysis
	6. Containment
Reactive	7. Communication
	8. Eradication
	9. Recovery
	10. Post-event analysis

Incident Response Team

The incident response team actively deploys during a cyber incident, but should have an established plan that they have practiced on a regular basis. The number of individuals involved in an incident response team is directly dependent on the size and structure of an organization. Nevertheless, most organizations will have a computer security incident response team (CSIRT), which comprises individuals in charge of coordinating the response to an attack.[16] The CSIRT is often led by an organization's chief information security officer, but will sometimes also be led by the COO or the CIO.

A CSIRT has several responsibilities before, during, and after a cyberattack, including:

- Understanding the operational impact of a cyberattack
- Acting as the central point for internal cyberattack reporting and communication
- Reporting to the relevant internal and external stakeholders when an incident arises

- Gathering forensic information for legal and analysis purposes
- Updating the incident response plan according to the changing threat landscape[17]

Cyber Crisis Communication Plan

This chapter's case study demonstrates that a key element of any cyberattack recovery is to make sure that communications with internal and external stakeholders are coordinated and effective. An appropriate cyber crisis communication plan helps mitigate several legal, operational, and reputational risks. A crisis communication plan has the potential to either contain or escalate the impact of an attack. For example, companies that fail to communicate properly with external stakeholders, including government agencies, investors, law enforcement, and customers, are at risk of legal action, which can lead to significant financial losses.[18]

Poor communications can also create panic and mistrust, causing reputational damage. Communication should, therefore, aim to restore trust and confidence in the organization and should outline what actions the company is taking to recover from the attack. Companies also need to adhere to state, national, and international reporting protocols and comply with cyberattack reporting processes. To do this, an organization needs to create a crisis communication plan that clearly outlines what communication processes need to be followed during an attack.

The Role of the Cyber Crisis Communication Plan

A cyber crisis communication plan ensures that the necessary stakeholders are provided with the appropriate information at the right time. It also ensures that the necessary notification processes are followed. When this is done, internal stakeholders are informed of any actions that need to be performed during the recovery stage. Likewise, external stakeholders are regularly informed about any new developments and how these impact them.[19]

It is important to remember that external stakeholders may not be familiar with the ramifications of an attack. For example, customers who are unfamiliar with cybersecurity issues may not be aware of the intricacies of an attack, such as the difference between an infrastructure breach and an information breach. As a result, crisis communications play a key role in ensuring that external stakeholders fully understand the significance of an attack by explaining the impact of a breach in an easily accessible and informative manner.

Both the incident response plan and the communications plan should be approved by an organization's CEO and the board of directors, and should be reviewed and updated on (at least) an annual basis.[20] The plan should detail the steps to be taken before, during, and after a cyberattack, and should be understood as an integrated, organization-wide plan, not something that is applicable only to the IT department.[21] It is therefore necessary that individuals from different departments, such as legal, human resources, public relations, facilities management, and operations, are involved in compiling this plan.

Going Deeper

The ten-step incident response process provides an excellent overarching framework for addressing key aspects of prevention and resilience.

Prevention

While ideally an organization could prevent cyberattacks altogether, such a goal is not realistic. Preventive measures only lower the probability of an attack; cyber risk can never be completely eliminated. Thus, all organizations need to have an incident response plan in place.

Planning

Similar to how an organization would put plans in place to deal with a power outage or natural disaster, it should have a plan to deal with the ramifications of a cyberattack. The advantages of planning in advance for an attack include the following:

- A systemic response can be taken in the event of an attack, which should minimize the human error that often results when decisions must be made under stressful circumstances.
- The implementation of a well-thought-out plan may reduce the losses suffered by the organization and minimize downtime.
- Evidence that a proper plan was in place and was followed will be useful should the attack lead to legal proceedings.[22]

The following actions should be taken during the planning phase:

- An incident response plan should be compiled and procedures should be documented.
- An incident response team should be appointed, consisting of individuals who have the necessary knowledge and experience to deal with a cyberattack. (Later on we'll say more about the different members included in an incident response team.)
- A cyber crisis communication plan should be compiled, detailing which parties should be contacted in case of an attack, the message that will be conveyed to them, and who has the authority to communicate on behalf of the organization. (Late on we will explore a suggested communication framework.)[23]

An incident response plan should serve as a roadmap, indicating how the organization will implement each step in the incident response process and who will be responsible for each task. Its aim is to ensure that the necessary people and tools are in place should a cyberattack occur, and that systematic and consistent actions are taken to minimize the risk to the organization. The organization will also benefit from the information obtained and recorded during the incident, which can then be used to improve its security measures and to prepare better for future incidents.

Preparation

Once an incident response plan has been completed, further preparations can be made to ensure that everyone is ready to implement the plan in the event of an attack.

Establish Reporting Mechanisms

Reporting mechanisms should be in place to ensure that employees can communicate an attack as quickly as possible to the correct person. (Later we'll cover communication and escalation plans in more detail.) The organization should decide whether all employees should have direct access to the response team, or whether employees should report incidents to their line managers, who will then escalate the matter on their behalf. Contingency plans should also be in place should line managers or response team members not be available.

Prepare Information Sheets and Checklists

Checklists that the incident response team must use during attacks should be prepared in advance to ensure that action can be taken swiftly, that tasks are not duplicated, and that no tasks are overlooked. High-level network diagrams and a list of critical assets should be prepared for the whole organization, so that the team can quickly see how the different systems are connected and how an attack might compromise these systems and networks. Often an organization neglects to compile these diagrams and lists of assets, especially when a substantial number of legacy components are in use. While documenting these assets could take time, it will be well worth the effort in the case of an attack. An issue tracking sheet or system should be prepared, which can be used to track the status of each task during incident response.[24] In addition to being stored securely, this should be printed out and placed in a secure place so that it can be accessed should all digital systems be inoperable.

Train the Response Team and Practice the Plan

Regular exercises should be conducted by the organization's incident response team, simulating a cyberattack. This will give the team an opportunity to identify actions that have to be taken, to test their plan, and to make changes to the processes if required.[25] Training exercises can take the following form:

- **Tabletop exercises:** Different scenarios of potential cyberattacks are created, and the incident response team has to answer questions relating to each scenario. The team then has to decide on the best response to each question. Their answers are reviewed to see whether the actions the team suggests are in line with the organization's incident response plan and general best practices. This is a relatively cheap and effective way to identify discrepancies or the need for additional procedures.[26]
- **War games:** The members of the incident response team take part in a game, based on a possible business scenario, that tests their knowledge and skills when it comes to handling a security incident. Each team is provided with certain information and must make practical decisions in a competitive environment to address the scenario they are presented with.[27]

Aside from conducting training exercises, the incident response team should conduct ongoing research to ensure that they stay up to date with the latest tools and technology available to deal with cyberattacks. They should also review industry trends and stay abreast of any new threats that have been reported in the media or that other information specialists are aware of.[28] This is called gathering threat intelligence.

It is impossible to train the response team to react to every type of threat, as new, previously unknown threats arise regularly. The focus should be on developing the basic capabilities of the team to respond to a variety of incidents, and to develop reporting chains and key team relationships that will assist the team in their response. Prioritizing organizational assets will also help to focus the response team's attention and capabilities on solving problems related to this core set of infrastructures.

Outsource Monitoring and Testing

An independent consultancy firm could be assigned to conduct audits on the readiness of the organization, which will highlight any areas for concern and provide the organization with feedback on processes that could still be improved.[29]

Third-party penetration testing could also be used to illuminate areas for improvement. There are two teams involved in this type of testing: a red team and a blue team. The red team is responsible for simulating an attack, while the blue team is responsible for stopping the attack.[30] The purpose of this exercise is to identify weak areas in the system and the response process.

Detection

A cyberattack cannot be dealt with until it has been detected, a lesson that Capital One learned the hard way. However, many cyberattacks occur over long periods of time and are often not detected until severe damage has been done. Detecting attacks is primarily a preventative measure, but we include it in this framework because of its obvious importance in incident response.

Analysis

Once a threat has been detected, it should be analyzed before any actions are taken. The most important reason for this analysis is to confirm whether an incident is actually an attack and not a false positive. Many alerts are generated daily, and the incident response team must determine which alerts are serious enough to spend time and resources on. IDPSs tend to signal false positives, which means it is necessary to examine the alerts generated by these systems and to find correlating evidence to determine whether any action is required.[31] This can be time-consuming, which is why many organizations have automated the initial analysis. Information can then be filtered to show only data that meets certain criteria, which is then further analyzed by humans to determine whether it poses a significant threat.

Incidents that are found to be valid do not necessarily indicate that a cyberattack is taking place. For example, the server might have crashed due to a malfunction instead of a cyberattack. The incident response team should ensure that any malfunctions have been ruled out before continuing their investigation.

Situational Awareness

Once it has been determined that the incident is not a false positive, the incident response team should conduct situational awareness. Situational awareness refers to investigating the extent and impact of an attack to make the correct decisions in time to decrease and eradicate the damage done by the attacker. It provides the organization with a better understanding of the incident and gives them an opportunity to verify information and make good decisions. Situational awareness is used to determine the extent of the impact, the type of attack, if any automated procedures were deployed to mitigate the attack internally, the networks and systems affected, the type of data that was breached (if any), the stage of the attack (if an attacker persists in the network), and the origin of the attack.

It is important to keep in mind that as much evidence as possible should be preserved during the analysis phase, as it might have to be used in future litigation.

Categorization

If more than one cyberattack is occurring at the same time, the attacks should be prioritized. Attacks should be categorized and prioritized based on the potential impact they may have on the organization and on the time and resources required to recover. Impact could include the impact the attack has on the functionality of the business, as well as the impact it has on the organization's information.[32]

Documentation

From the moment that an incident has been validated as a cyber-attack, everything relating to the attack should be documented. These documents will serve as a reference when post-event analysis is performed, and as evidence in legal proceedings. The following should be documented:

- A short explanation of what happened
- How the incident was detected, who reported the incident, and whether they were alerted manually or by an automated system
- The steps taken by individuals from the detection of the event right through to the recovery stage
- The status of the incident as it moves through the recovery process
- Any evidence that is gathered during the process that can be used to determine who the attacker was
- Any comments and suggestions from the incident response team[33]

Once the information and situation have been properly analyzed, the team can move on to containing the attack.

Containment

The purpose of containment is to stop the attack from spreading to other systems or departments within the organization, and to limit the amount of damage done.[34] It also provides the incident response team with some time to decide on the next steps to take.

It might be that the threat was contained automatically by the IDPS or a virus removal program, which means that no further action is required from the incident response team and they can move on to the next step in the process. However, if no automated actions were taken, the affected systems should be identified and one of the following steps implemented (depending on the situation):

- Isolate the affected device from the network by blocking connectivity, if operationally possible.
- Shut down systems and reroute components.
- Disable some functions performed by systems.
- Shut down communication to the infected area. This is not always recommended, however, as threats already contained in an environment can be monitored and followed, so that you can learn more about their potential impact if detected elsewhere in the network.[35]

The action taken depends on whether some services still have to be available to the organization's employees or customers, and whether a short- or long-term solution is required until the team can eradicate the threat.

Backups should be made of all infected systems for forensic purposes before the threat is contained. It may be necessary to move very quickly through the response process, which means that the response team must weigh the advantages of preserving evidence against the damage done if the threat is not contained immediately.

Communication

Ensuring proper communications during an attack is perhaps the most important element of enabling organizational resilience. There are a number of considerations when establishing communication during a crisis, and this requires a crisis communication plan. As part of a crisis communication plan, provisions should be made for communicating with both external and internal stakeholders over secure media.

Communicating with Key External Stakeholders

Because of the far-reaching impact of a cyberattack, external stakeholders need to be informed of a breach and how it impacts them. Nevertheless, before an incident occurs, the CSIRT needs to discuss information-sharing criteria with their public relations specialist, the legal team, and senior management.[36] These discussions establish important information-sharing criteria that will be documented in the crisis communication plan (Table 7.2).

Before communicating with external stakeholders, it is important to consult legal counsel when sharing information externally about a hack, as the organization might open itself up to legal damages.

Regardless of the stakeholders an organization is communicating with, the information given should be clearly stated. Ambiguity and incorrect messaging lead to confusion and can result in legal action.

Communicating with Internal Stakeholders

Communication within the organization is just as important as external communication. This is because internal staff are most often the closest touchpoints between an organization and its customers. As a result, internal staff need to be kept abreast of important developments so that they can clearly communicate with affected parties, helping to restore confidence.

While it may not be possible to relay all the information relating to a cyberattack to internal employees, senior management should ensure that they share enough information with their staff to instill confidence. Staff should also be informed of what information they are permitted to share with customers publicly. Likewise, senior management should inform staff if employees' personal information has been compromised. Employees need to be reassured that their information is being protected along with customer information.[37]

Channels of Communication

To ensure effective internal communication, clear lines of communication need to be established. These forms of official communication are typically broken down into three types of communication: upward, downward, and horizontal.[38] Upward communication should be concise and should only provide the necessary technical details that are required for the relevant stakeholders. Downward communication, on the other hand, should be reassuring and as informative as possible based on the information that needs to be communicated downward. Horizontal communication mainly serves to enhance

Table 7.2 Communication Strategies for Key External Stakeholders

Communication Strategies for Key External Stakeholders	
The media	Communication with the media should be informed by company media policies and information disclosure requirements. It is important that all media communication comes from a senior executive of the company, to highlight the seriousness of the issue.
Law enforcement	Prior to an attack, the CSIRT must determine what legal requirements need to be met, which law enforcement officials should be contacted, and under what circumstances these officials should be notified of a cyberattack. These variables will depend on the nature of possible attacks, as well as the jurisdictions of both the organization and its customers. As part of incident response preparation, the CSIRT should have established how reporting with law enforcement will be conducted, what information will be shared, and what evidence will be collected.[*]
Incident reporting organizations	Not all countries have the same organizations to assist during a cyberattack. However, in the United States, federal agencies are required to report cyberattacks to the United States Computer Emergency Readiness Team (US-CERT), which has been established to help facilitate incident handling.[*] An organization may also be required to report a breach to the Securities and Exchange Commission if the breach impacts its bottom line. Some industries have set up information sharing and analysis centers to help promote information sharing between private organizations. By establishing a relationship with the relevant ISAC, the CSIRT will have access to additional support during an attack. The Forum for Incident Response and Security Teams (FIRST) and the Government Forum of Incident Response and Security Teams (GFIRST) are both alternative organizations that aim to facilitate knowledge sharing that increases incident preparedness.[*]
Impacted external parties	Other impacted external parties that need to be notified include owners of attacking addresses whose computers may be being used to conduct the hack, software vendors, customers, external suppliers, internet service providers, and other affected parties whose sensitive information may have been hacked. Publicly traded companies in the United States are required to disclose in their annual report the risk of cyberattacks occurring, if the costs or risks involved with these attacks are likely to have a material impact on the company's financial results.[**]

[*] Cichonski, P., T. Millar, T. Grance, and K. Scarfone. 2012. "Computer Security Incident Handling Guide—Recommendations of the National Institute of Standards and Technology." NIST Special Publication 800-61 Revision 2. https://csrc.nist.gov/publications/detail/sp/800-61/rev-2/final.

[**] U.S. Securities and Exchange Commission. 2011. "CF Disclosure Guidance: Topic No. 2." https://www.sec.gov/divisions/corpfin/guidance/cfguidance-topic2.htm.

coordination between teams and departments, and therefore tends to be more practical and technical in nature.

During a cyberattack, it is important that all staff members are aware of the appropriate channels of communication that need to be used. These relationships define who reports to whom and the communication hierarchy.[39] Individual team members need to know whom to report an issue to and feel empowered to notify superiors of irregularities.

Escalation Strategies

Internal communication plans should also include escalation strategies that outline exactly how team members need to respond and whom they should notify in the event of a cyberattack. This is especially important if a cyberattack impacts outside stakeholders. If this is the case, team members need to know which legal, human resource, and media personnel need to be informed to help manage expectations and share information about the actions being taken to recover from the breach.

Eradication

Eradication refers to identifying the root cause of a cyberattack and eliminating it.[40] This will ensure that the environment is secure in order for recovery processes to begin. It might be necessary to use forensic software to identify the root of the problem (and the party responsible for launching the attack) before it can be eradicated. The incident response team is responsible for identifying the attack vector and the path of the attack to ensure that all entry points are closed and that infected areas are cleaned up.[41] Involvement from individuals within the affected business units might also be necessary to ensure that all vectors are eradicated.

Persistence is generally a feature of sophisticated attacks, meaning that the attack vector has self-preservation capabilities and intends to stealthily stay on the machine even after cleanup. Because of this, extra care must be taken to evaluate any places attack vectors could be hiding to maintain persistence. This might mean revisiting the detection and analysis steps in the process to ensure that all threats have been identified. Any weak areas identified during the eradication phase should be strengthened to prevent the same or similar attacks from occurring again, whether as a result of persistence or from an entirely new malware attack that uses similar attack vectors. This could take the form of strategic fixes, but it should also be remembered when long-term improvements are made to the system as part of an entire network overhaul.[42]

The following steps should be taken during eradication, depending on the type and nature of the attack:[43]

- Scan systems for latent malware, and remove malware using tools such as antivirus software.
- Isolate and disable accounts and components that have been breached.
- Remove access privileges from employees who were used as a means to launch the attack.
- Change usernames and passwords to close attack vectors to the network.
- Apply patches and reconfigure firewalls.

Once the threat has been eradicated, the recovery process can begin.

Recognize that there might be tension between the need to get systems up and running again as soon as possible and the need to ensure that all traces of the attack have been eliminated before recovery begins.

Recovery

Recovery refers to the organization's systems' return to full working order. This process usually takes some time and is not a one-off action. Different stakeholders from across the organization (ranging from the IT department and the affected business units to the operations department and senior management) are involved in the recovery process. These stakeholders could either be directly involved in the recovery process or provide guidance regarding the process to follow and the time frames that should be adhered to. The systems that are the most important for the business to resume basic functionality should be prioritized. The interdependencies between systems should also be understood, as some systems can only be recovered after others have been restored.

Once the attack can be attributed to a specific group or individual, it might be easier to recover from the attack, as the incident response team will have a better understanding of the motivation for the attack and the methods used.[44] Advanced persistent threat (APT) attacks, for example, are most often carried out by nation-states due to the number of resources required.

During recovery, systems are rebuilt, reinstalled, or restored by the incident recovery team using backup data. Files are replaced with clean versions, and patches are installed. It is important that the recovered systems are tested and monitored to ensure that reinfection does not take place, and that they are functioning the way they are supposed to.[45] The recovery process is an opportunity to enhance security based on the vulnerabilities that were discovered during the detection and analysis steps.

Because the recovery process could potentially take months, it has become necessary for organizations to ensure that they are operationally resilient. This refers to the ability to operate with diminished system capacity.[46] Business continuity plans, service-level agreements with vendors (to ensure immediate access to the necessary hardware and software), and proactive communication with stakeholders (such as customers) are some elements that could make a business more cyber resilient, and should therefore be included in the incident response plan.

Post-Incident Analysis

It is necessary to assess a cyberattack after it occurred to determine whether or not the response to the attack was sufficient and to implement lessons learned. This step might kick off while recovery is still ongoing, particularly if it takes a while for all systems to be recovered. The aim of this step is to improve the incident response plan and to strengthen systems to protect them from future attacks.

Lessons-Learned Meeting

A lessons-learned meeting should be held as soon as possible after the attack occurred, and should be attended by all parties involved in the incident.[47] The aim of this meeting is to identify any deficiencies in how the detection and eradication of the attack were handled. Another lessons-learned meeting should also take place after systems have been fully recovered. This is meant to sufficiently capture lessons about the general recovery process, and about how the organization must further improve its operational resilience.

Incident Report

An incident report (also called a post-mortem report) should be compiled after the conclusion of the lessons-learned meeting. This report not only will serve as a reference to plan for future attacks, but also will be useful as a training tool going forward. In addition, it can be used as evidence should any legal matters arise due to the attack.

The report should address:[48]

- The type and nature of the incident
- Whether or not the incident could have been prevented
- How and when the incident was detected, and whether any improvements to detection tools are required
- The systems affected by the attack
- How the organization responded to the attack, and what could have been done better during the incident response process
- Recommendations to improve the response process going forward

Complete the Improvement Feedback Loop

All the lessons learned from the post-event analysis should now be implemented to reduce the risk of future incidents occurring, and to ensure that the organization is better prepared should an attack take place again. Changes may have to be made to policies, processes, and procedures, to tools and equipment, and even to the behavior of the parties involved in the process.

Improvements should be categorized as short-term or long-term.[49] Short-term improvements can be made immediately, while long-term improvements relate to strategic changes, such as completely redesigning certain processes, that will take longer to implement. Action plans that include responsible parties, due dates, and deliverables should be created to ensure that all stakeholders know what is expected of them. The updated and improved incident response plan should also be tested before it is rolled out to determine whether the improvements made are sufficient.

Taking Action

Executing an incident response process will require a coordinated response from various parts of the organization. The two actions you can take to prepare include assembling your CSIRT and developing your crisis communication plan.

Preparing Your Incident Response Team

To enable organizational resilience in the face of an attack, the correct stakeholders and team members across departments, such as management, IT, operations, legal, and marketing, all need to be empowered to act as part of the CSIRT team. These individuals need to be familiar with the incident response strategy and should have rehearsed the necessary procedures.

Identify the CSIRT Command Structure

An organization can choose to structure their CSIRT in two ways—as a central CSIRT or as a distributed CSIRT. The choice depends on the scale, structure, and culture of the organization, as follows:

1. **Central CSIRT:** A centralized team handles all cyberattack issues throughout the organization. This allows for quick and coordinated responses, but it may not work in larger organizational contexts, like multinational organizations.[50]
2. **Distributed CSIRT:** A distributed CSIRT would result in several smaller response teams established throughout the organization with their own unique responsibilities. These smaller teams form part of the larger CSIRT. This model is appropriate for large organizations that have offices in different locations, like Unilever and General Motors.[51]

Identify Key Actors and Their Role

The contact details and responsibilities of each CSIRT member should be widely circulated within the organization as part of the incident response planning process. The CSIRT can include internal and external stakeholders, and may consist of the following members (Table 7.3):
It is crucial to define the scope and responsibilities of each CSIRT member before, during, and after a cyberattack. This provides clarity and direction when team members need to act quickly.

Preparing Your Cyber Crisis Communication Plan

One point that Capital One CEO Richard Fairbank understood was the importance of communication after the attack was discovered. Amid the potential chaos of an attack, it is critical to have a clear plan for how the organization will communicate to its various stakeholders about the crisis. Crisis communication has the potential to contain the reputational, legal, and operational risks of a breach, or it can inflame the situation, causing confusion and, in some cases, significant financial losses.

The plan needs to outline key communication procedures that will be followed during an attack (Table 7.4). Without a crisis communication plan in place, stakeholders with the expertise to mitigate an

Table 7.3 Key Actors

Key Actors	
CISO	The CISO is responsible for the security of the organization's information assets (although the CEO bears ultimate accountability) and is generally a member of the executive committee. The CSIRT reports to and works closely with the CISO.
Team manager	The team manager coordinates the entire CSIRT and must be empowered by senior management to act on behalf of the company. The team manager also manages all external consultants and subcontractors.
Control system engineer	The control system engineer is a subject-matter expert who has a detailed understanding of the control system architecture. This team member should be familiar with the operational impact of an attack and how an organization can work around any system failures.
Network administrator	The network administrator is an expert on network access and security vulnerabilities. This team member has access to information about activity logs before, during, and after an attack, which would be used to determine the scope and impact of a breach.
System administrator	The system administrator has a deep understanding of access permissions and system operation logs on all servers. This team member is able to identify potential vulnerabilities and how the hack impacts company systems. When external vendors are used, this team member assists the team manager and acts as an intermediary.
Operations manager	The operations manager has the authority to stop operations in the event of an attack. This team member is a key touchpoint between the CSIRT, the COO, and senior management. The operations manager may also deal with communications with external stakeholders and the media, and should be involved in the risk assessment process.
IT director	The IT director has responsibilities similar to the operations manager's, and must coordinate with the operations manager to divert resources and delegate responsibilities.
General counsel or legal experts	The general counsel or an external legal expert should assist with issues of compliance with state, national, and international laws, industry regulations, privacy violations, and liability exposure.
Security experts	These individuals can include law enforcement, physical security representatives, and cybersecurity experts. These experts have in-depth knowledge of cyberattacks and prevention techniques, and are invaluable during the recovery process.

Continued

Table 7.3 Continued

Key Actors	
Public relations specialists	A public relations specialist ensures that the necessary information is communicated clearly to the relevant parties via various media channels. This team member ensures that information-sharing criteria are met and that external communication is coordinated.
Human resources specialists	The HR specialist is involved if an attack is conducted by an employee. This team member assists with policies and procedures as well as any legal issues.
Support staff	A list of additional support staff should be created if further expertise is required. These individuals may be forensics experts, law enforcement personnel, government agencies, platform specialists, or application developers. The contact details of these individuals should be easy to access and widely circulated.
Vendor support staff	Vendor support staff can be used to provide technical support with any equipment or system faults. They may have unique knowledge that helps if custom patches need to be created during the recovery process for key assets.[*]
Insurer	The cyber insurance provider or broker can play a role in helping to coordinate the various external parties after an attack. Often, insurance covers certain response services, and the insurer may have existing relationships with preferred providers that are on retainer and can be readily engaged.

[*] U.S. Department of Homeland Security. 2009. *"Recommended Practice: Developing an Industrial Control System Cybersecurity Incident Response Capability."* https://ics-cert.us-cert.gov/sites/default/files/recommended_practices/final-RP_ics_cybersecurity_incident_response_100609.pdf.

attack may not be notified in time, delaying the recovery process.[52] The organization also opens itself up to legal and regulatory risks if it fails to notify key parties in a timely manner.

Establish Alternative Communication Mediums

Preparing alternative communication channels in advance is a useful method of ensuring quick communication between internal and external stakeholders when there is a cyber crisis. By establishing alternative websites especially designed for crisis communication and other channels of communication, an organization will be better prepared to take charge of the situation—especially if traditional channels are compromised as a result of the attack.

Table 7.4 The Elements of a Cyber Crisis Communication Plan

The Elements of a Cyber Crisis Communication Plan	
Communication objectives	Given the resource and time constraints that a cyber crisis can impose, it is important to itemize and rank your objectives in order of priority.
Stakeholder information and contact details	Ensure that stakeholder information and contact details are maintained and updated regularly, while recognizing that access to your first-choice channel (such as email) may be limited in a cyber crisis.
Internal and external communication considerations	Considerations tend to vary greatly depending on the specific organizational context, such as your sector and your organizational culture.
Information-sharing criteria	During a cyber crisis, too much information can become as crippling as too little. Clear, objective thresholds for what information to provide to which stakeholders will help your organization make the best use of its communication channels.
Internal upward communication processes	Internal upward communication should optimize for brevity, providing only the necessary technical details for the relevant stakeholders.
Internal downward communication processes	Communication from management to employees should be informative and reassuring to the extent possible.
Stakeholder notification processes[*]	This does not require a separate plan for each individual stakeholder. Consider grouping stakeholders into categories (such as "media," "online customers," and "account holders") that streamline this process.

[*] Cichonski, P., T. Millar, T. Grance, and K. Scarfone. 2012. "Computer Security Incident Handling Guide." NIST Special Publications 800-61 Revision 2. http://nvlpubs.nist. gov/nistpubs/SpecialPublications/NIST.SP.800-61r2.pdf; Kral, P. 2011. "The Incident Handlers Handbook." SANS. https://www.sans.org/reading-room/whitepapers/incident/incident-handlers-handbook-33901.

Action on the Front Lines

As we've explained in this chapter, mitigating the consequences of a successful cyberattack requires an organization to prepare for the worst with an incident response plan. Capital One CEO Richard Fairbank was an anomaly: he both prepped his organization with a response plan before the attack and took responsibility after it occurred. Fairbank's leadership stands in stark contrast to the truly pathetic failure by Equifax CEO Richard Smith in response to the hack of his organization.

Many CEOs fail to prioritize their personal involvement in incident response planning because they don't believe it's worth the investment of their time. It's true that a CEO's time is very valuable, but, as Rosenbach likes to tell corporate executives, if the president of the United States and eighty-five senators can make time to actively participate in cyber incident response planning and exercises, so can you![53]

Throughout 2012, Rosenbach supported efforts led by the White House to craft and execute a national-level exercise to prepare the United States government for a response to a potential catastrophic cyberattack on the nation's electric grid. After months of staff-level planning, the effort started with a classified exercise provided by cabinet-level leaders for the U.S. Senate, which many of the senators attended. The results of the exercise? One leading senator told the participants, "This scared the pants off me, not just because of the scenario, but because I see that President Obama's administration is woefully underprepared to respond to an attack."

With that in mind, during the summer of 2012, President Obama actively participated in the planning exercise, which included a meeting of the full cabinet for several hours to role-play the response to the simulated attack. The response plan was complex: it included options for private-sector collaboration, nationwide public communications and alerts, and even a full-blown plan for military action against the fictional rogue nation that had attacked America. The execution of the national incident response plan was far from perfect, but rehearsing the plan allowed the government to highlight areas of weakness and further prepare for a real-world event.

Main Takeaway

The amount of planning an organization has put into its incident response plan determines, in part, how resilient it will be after a cyberattack. Following the ten steps in the incident response process provides structure and preparation in advance of a potentially chaotic scenario. Part of this preparation includes gathering the correct individuals with the necessary skills to form an organization's CSIRT. This team needs to be empowered to act quickly, leveraging relevant tools at their disposal. Clear communication with both external and internal stakeholders also significantly impacts the recovery process. Poor communication can delay action, create confusion, and significantly damage an organization's reputation. Embedded Endurance is fundamentally about the ability to persist in the face of adversity. Empowering the organization with a clear plan to identify what happened, return to some semblance of normal operations, and evaluate what could be done better next time facilitates the organization's resilience to a cyberattack.

8

How Do I Embed Cyber Risk Management in All Aspects of the Organization?

Adopting an Embedded Endurance strategy

Case Study

The 2017 NotPetya cyberattack shocked executives worldwide, and the leaders of Mondelez International were no exception. Even so, it was ultimately the actions of its own insurance provider that most surprised the multinational snack food giant.

What Happened?

NotPetya malware rendered 1,700 of Mondelez's servers and 24,000 of its laptops "permanently dysfunctional."[1] Facing over $100 million in damage,[2] Mondelez submitted a claim covering these losses to its insurer, Zurich Insurance. Mondelez's policy covered "physical loss or damage to electronic data, programs, or software, including physical loss or damage caused by the malicious introduction of a machine code or instruction."[3] The policy also covered extra expenses incurred during the associated interruption.[4]

But Zurich refused to pay.

Confronting Cyber Risk. Gregory Falco and Eric Rosenbach, Oxford University Press. © Oxford University Press 2022. DOI: 10.1093/oso/9780197526545.003.0008

The company argued it had not insured Mondelez against damages incurred by war, and this was an act of cyberwar.[5] More specifically, Zurich denied Mondelez's claim based on a policy exclusion for "hostile or warlike activities" by a government or an agent acting on its behalf.[6] Mondelez denounced Zurich's move as "unprecedented" and responded by suing its insurer for the full $100 million in damages.[7]

The Impact

Mondelez endured a clear business impact as a result of this cyberattack. It was able to make a cohesive claim to its insurer because the company had identified its critical systems, networks, and data and was able to judge the attack's impact on those systems. Developing a business impact analysis enabled Mondelez to approach its insurer with substantiated data about the losses incurred.

By identifying its assets and characterizing the types of cyberattacks that could compromise these assets, Mondelez was able to make a robust claim to Zurich. However, this situation demonstrates the importance of an Embedded Endurance strategy: cyber risks should not only be considered at the level of either individual devices or the organization's overarching structure, but instead addressed throughout every aspect of the organization. Unfortunately, in this case, Mondelez only sought the catch-all defense strategy of insurance—which does not always work out as expected.

Zurich's response to the claim is an example of how certain mitigation measures of your risk management plan may not yield the expected result (i.e., the insurance payout), regardless of your plan's depth and breadth. Embedding resilience at every level of the organization is required.

Preparing You to Do Better

While cyber insurance potentially offers a way to shield your organization from the financial impact of a cyber incident, the Mondelez case demonstrates that it does not always work out as planned. This illustrates the necessity of an Embedded Endurance strategy—one in which prevention and resilience techniques are infused across every aspect of the organization, at the micro and macro levels, thereby minimizing the impact of an attack.

Why It Matters

As organizations become more dependent on information and operational technology, the risk of a cyber incident grows. This increases the need to address these risks holistically and plan accordingly. This reinforces the need for Embedded Endurance, which integrates all aspects of cyber risk mitigation and enables an organization to comprehensively address cyber risks and their potential impact on operations, reputation, and legal liability. Embedded Endurance takes the long view of cyber risk rather than engaging in hyper-reactive changes to an organization's cyber risk management plan each time there is an incident.

Key Concept

1. Risk management strategy's importance

Risk Management Strategy's Importance

A risk management strategy encourages an organization to prioritize its risks so that it devotes resources only to significant threats.[8] It also allows an organization to define action plans and to assign responsibility for the implementation of those plans to specific individuals. Creating a risk management strategy that includes clear goals, objectives, and milestones—as well as metrics to measure whether goals have been met—will ensure that cybersecurity remains a top priority.

The book has covered a lot of ground. Due to both the diversity of organizations for which cyber risk is critical and the plethora of cyber threats that exist, some elements will be more relevant to you than others. Your performance as a leader managing your organization's cyber risk depends on how you piece together the insights outlined in this book, augment them with your own experience and knowledge, and tailor a strategy to the unique profile of your organization.

Because this chapter aims to help you establish an Embedded Endurance cyber risk management strategy, we aggregate key elements from each chapter relevant to this end. Think of it not only as an opportunity to refresh your memory of the content, but also as a chance to broaden your understanding of the interconnections among the various elements of Embedded Endurance.

Going Deeper

Embedding Endurance

Your digital organization is composed of many interdependent socio-technical systems, all of which are vulnerable to cyberattack. The cheapest option may be to deploy some technology to plug obvious security holes, but Band-Aids inevitably fall off. Each interdependent system's security will falter at some point, but no single digital asset or individual alone makes for an organization's success; what's important is the whole of your organization's socio-technical mesh. Embedding security at each level of the organization—be it through employee education or antivirus heuristics—will enable you to succeed in the indefinite process of cyber risk management.

If nothing else, this chapter's case study should convince you that managing cyber risk can be a messy and unpredictable process, thereby necessitating a comprehensive Embedded Endurance strategy. Thus, while any book on managing cyber risk is necessarily linear, the reality is far more iterative. The business impact analysis your organization conducts may push you to reconsider which cyber threat actors you target. The risk prevention and resilience measures at your disposal may affect how various cyber laws and standards apply to you. In short, it is worth reviewing the key features of each chapter that will help to inform your Embedded Endurance strategy. Consult the summaries in what follows and refer back to any of the chapters for which a more comprehensive review may help:

- **Chapter 1, "Why is cyber risk an issue?":** Given the constant presence of threat actors, cyberattacks against private and public organizations are inevitable. Because attackers face relatively little risk compared to the potential losses that the organizations they target could suffer, hackers have an advantage over those targeted. Thus, cyber risk management is a nonstop process, but you can take immediate steps to improve your organization's Embedded Endurance.

- **Chapter 2, "Who is attacking us?":** Not all hackers are alike, and it is important to understand who might attack your organization and how they might strike. Because different sectors often appeal to hackers for very different reasons, your team's risk management measures are strongest when taking these unique circumstances into account.

- **Chapter 3, "How do I assess our cyber risk?":** Assessing cyber risk is more than simply listing vulnerabilities and prognosticating the odds of a major attack. It requires conducting a complete business impact analysis so that you can assess the types of damage incurred in a cyberattack and prioritize your responses in the face of limited time and resources. Identifying which of your organization's systems, networks, and data are truly critical is impossible without first understanding how they relate to each other and how they serve your business priorities.

- **Chapter 4, "What do I need to know about cyber frameworks, standards, and laws?":** When thinking about cybersecurity, many forget the importance of legal obligations and industry standards. However, the financial and reputational costs associated with legal non-compliance alone justify making cyber risk management part of an organization's overall risk management strategy. Executives must be aware of the various sources of legal requirements and industry benchmarks—including state law, federal law, and industry bodies—and adopt a strategy responsive to legal compliance risks.

- **Chapter 5, "Who is responsible for cybersecurity?"**: Managing organizational cyber risk starts at the top, with the CEO and board of directors. From there, all business users should know their cyber risk management role(s) and engage in the effort. Without everyone playing their part, vulnerabilities in the organization's cyber risk posture will inevitably arise.

- **Chapter 6, "What risk prevention measures can I use?"**: Risk prevention tools and procedures are fundamental to preventing incidents and minimizing the impact of those that occur. Given the finite resources an organization can deploy to these ends in a fiscal cycle, leadership should select prevention mechanisms based on the systems, networks, and data prioritization defined through the BIA.

- **Chapter 7, "What risk resilience measures can I use?"**: A clear incident response process provides structure and preparation for handling the chaos and confusion that a hack may create, thereby minimizing its impact and enabling business continuity. For most organizations a key response component is the formation of a computer security incident response team that is empowered to act quickly. A clear plan to identify what happened, return to (somewhat) normal operations, and evaluate how to improve facilitates the organization's resilience to a cyberattack.

Taking Action

Strategy development is difficult for any challenge, but the extent of exposure any organization has to digital risk makes developing a strategy particularly thorny. Following a disciplined strategy development process, however, will help you build out an effective Embedded Endurance strategy that suits your organization's unique needs.

In what follows we outline the most important steps for developing your own strategy, which include:

- Starting with an established framework to guide the strategy development process, crafting a vision statement for the strategy
- Setting achievable goals and further breaking these down into definable objectives
- Determining actions and associated milestones, establishing metrics to measure progress toward objectives
- Continuously reviewing progress and taking steps toward improving the risk management strategy
- Most important, determining who has ultimate responsibility for strategy execution.

Start with a Framework

The most effective leaders use heuristics or conceptual frameworks to guide their strategy development processes. As mentioned earlier in this book, the best example of a useful tool in the cyber risk context is the National Institute of Standards and Technology's Cybersecurity Framework, developed to guide private-sector organizations in assessing their capacity to effectively manage cyber risks. Over the past decade, countless organizations have turned to the NIST Cybersecurity Framework to guide their strategy development process. For example, after the historic cyberattack that Saudi Aramco suffered in 2012, the organization used the framework to guide its strategy and cybersecurity maturity efforts.

Develop a Vision Statement

The leader of the organization should work with key stakeholders to craft a single statement that identifies what the organization wants to achieve with the implementation of the cyber risk management strategy. To develop your vision statement, start by thinking about the next five to ten years, then describe a picture of success. The vision statement should be linked to the organization's overall mission statement in a discernible way, and an effective leader will reference it often in communications and the implementation process.

Set Strategic Goals

While a vision encompasses the intention of the strategy, strategic goals help to ground the vision in your organization's risks. An example of a strategic goal could be, for example, to create a culture of cybersecurity awareness in the organization.

After the strategic goals have been identified, they must be prioritized, as the organization will likely not have the time and resources available to achieve all goals in the short term. The aim is to identify goals that are non-negotiable and that must be achieved for the organization to remain resilient in the face of an attack.

Define Measurable Objectives

Each strategic goal should include a set of objectives that, if followed, will help to achieve the strategic goal. They should be thought of as "to-dos" or "action items" that will result in meeting the strategic goal. For example, if one of the strategic goals of an organization is to protect its systems using technology, one of several objectives could be to implement and configure an intrusion detection system. The most effective objectives are specific, measurable, and achievable.

Craft an Action Plan
with Clear Milestones

An action plan involves assigning individuals or teams to the objectives, while also determining a timeline to accomplish the objectives. Milestones are set in order to reflect on progress and determine if the defined pathway forward still makes sense based on recent events. Action plans are critical, as they not only assign responsibility, but also can dictate accountability in cases with established and monitorable success criteria.

The vision sets the scene for the strategy, while the strategic goals are the high-level aspects on which the organization will focus. The objectives provide more detailed information about the steps that will be taken to achieve the strategic goals, while the action plans allocate time and resources toward the achievement of the objectives. By including these elements, the organization evolves from planning risk mitigation to executing practical steps that address the risks.

Establish Concrete Metrics

In order to evaluate whether success criteria are being met, elements of the plan must be monitored using both quantitative and qualitative methods and associated metrics. Sometimes metrics need to be developed based on your organization's unique context and actions; in other situations, metrics can be standard across organizations.

For example, if the objective is for all staff members in the organization to partake in cybersecurity awareness training during a specific period, the metric could be the number of staff members who successfully completed the training at the end of the period. If the objective is to have strong passwords on all computers to prevent unauthorized access, the metric could be the number of weak passwords identified during an audit.

Continuous Improvement Monitoring Process

Leadership should have visibility into an organization's Embedded Endurance strategy and monitor its progress using the defined metrics. As objectives are being met, it is critical for leadership to acknowledge the accomplishment and then to evolve the strategy, setting new milestones and establishing additional strategic goals where necessary to continuously improve the organization. Components of the risk management strategy that are faltering based on the defined metrics should be assessed and other approaches for achieving the strategic goals should be considered. Finally, leadership should hold those responsible for the various objectives accountable for missed objectives, or conversely celebrate them when they achieve objectives. Leadership should also host regular feedback sessions with relevant stakeholders. Threat actors are continuously evolving and improving their techniques to disrupt your organization; thus, your organization needs to continuously improve to stay one step ahead. Cyber risk mitigation is a matter of *endurance.*

Leadership, Leadership, Leadership

Due to the complexities involved in the implementation of an Embedded Endurance strategy, an organization should appoint a leader who is responsible for the development and implementation of the strategy. This person should have the necessary skills and expertise to address the challenges that arise, and should have the authority to ensure that the strategy becomes a practical reality instead of just a paper exercise.

While developing a concerted cyber risk management strategy document can align stakeholders on your unique Embedded Endurance strategy, it is important to remember that Embedded Endurance is about infusing all aspects of the organization with cyber risk management. The strategy is ineffective if siloed in a single department or exclusively engaged with by the CIO's office alone. Embedded Endurance can help ensure that your organization is prepared to face cyber adversaries over the long haul, limiting the opportunity for a single misstep to result in an incident that upends your entire organization. Such a pervasive approach requires strong leadership to drive the strategy across the organization.

Challenges When Implementing an Embedded Endurance Strategy

One of the biggest challenges in creating an Embedded Endurance strategy is communicating its importance to an organization's leadership and ensuring organizational buy-in. In this regard, the introduction to the strategy should set out to convey a high-level overview of the organization's need for a risk management strategy. It should provide enough context so that anyone reading the strategy will have a basic understanding of the purpose it aims to achieve.

Depending on the requirements of an organization's Embedded Endurance strategy, leaders may face several pitfalls during implementation. Management should be aware of the challenges associated with implementation, including compliance, collaboration, allocating financial resources, allocating human resources, assigning appropriate metrics, and handling the dynamic operating environment.[9]

Action on the Front Lines

Embedded Endurance is purpose-built as a multilayered cyber risk management approach for a world in which multiple issues can occur simultaneously. Depending so heavily on any one aspect of your organization's defenses—as Mondelez did with its insurance—can create the potential for disaster. Given this reality, leaders should focus on the development and execution of an Embedded Endurance strategy that layers numerous prevention and resilience measures to protect their organization's mission-critical assets and processes. Cyber risk permeates every aspect of an organization and its policy.

In 2015, the Department of Defense published its first-ever actionable cyber strategy. Rosenbach, who at the time served as an assistant secretary of defense and the "cyber czar" for the department, led the drafting process, which took more than eighteen months. As described previously, the strategy started with a vision statement from the secretary of defense, and included strategic goals and measurable objectives.[10]

What distinguished the strategy from other analogous documents in government or the private sector is that Rosenbach used the strategy to drive all of the department's work on cyber issues over the next two years. This included a governance process that forced all of the senior leaders in the department to report their progress quarterly in meetings with the secretary of defense and the chairman of the Joint Chiefs of Staff. Rather than write a document that would simply collect dust on the top shelf of offices at military bases around the world, Rosenbach and the truly exceptional leadership team around him made the strategy a well-thumbed guide to improving the military's cyber readiness and security posture.

The importance of a well-conceived strategy was particularly apparent to Falco when he consulted for the World Bank Group, working with thought leaders and national regulatory authorities from the Kingdom of Saudi Arabia as they established regulations for autonomous vehicles. Autonomous vehicle regulation involves a wide variety of components such as safety, roadside infrastructure, insurance, and data management. Each component of the regulation being developed for the kingdom includes a cyber risk consideration, thereby truly embedding cyber endurance into regulatory policy. There was never a question of where in the regulatory value chain cyber risk was most critical—cyber risk response and resilience were necessarily embedded across every component of the program.

Sometimes it takes longer to realize that an Embedded Endurance strategy is necessary. When Falco worked with officials and consultants who were crafting cybersecurity strategy for the country of Iceland, he saw that their initial approach to cyber risk was entirely reactive, relying heavily on foreign expertise, tools, and services. This appropriately reflects the country's national motto: *Þetta reddast*, which translates to "It will all work out okay." As Iceland noticed an uptick in attacks and engaged in cyber strategy-building workshops over the past years, the country has shifted its stance on cyber risk management. Its new strategy places importance on in-country cybersecurity education, thereby fostering an emergent generation of cyber risk professionals, while also amplifying its financial investment in cyber risk management to account for society's growing digital threats. While this may seem like a subtle change, it signifies a mindset shift toward an Embedded Endurance strategy, rather than one of persistent troubleshooting.

Main Takeaway

Establishing and acting on an Embedded Endurance strategy requires weaving together the various cybersecurity mechanisms at the disposal of leaders. The strategy helps to focus management's attention on the areas in their organization that need improvement and prioritize actions accordingly. It also serves as a guideline for all stakeholders and provides management with the means to measure the progress made in preparing the organization for a cyberattack. By developing an Embedded Endurance strategy unique to your organization that documents the compendium of cyber risk goals, measurable objectives, and an action plan that facilitates continuous improvement, leadership can define a "true north" to orient their risk prevention efforts and build resilience in the face of persistent cyber threats.

Conclusion

Cyber risk is not a static problem; at no point can you definitively say, "We have it all covered." This is largely a function of cyber risk being a systems challenge in which digital assets are highly interdependent, each with its own dynamic risk profile. Approaching cyber risk with a systems engineering mindset, which is inherent to the Embedded Endurance strategy, will thus help your organization map the scope of its risk and evaluate its options.

Regardless of the investment an organization may make in cyber risk management, there is always some creative attacker assessing the possibilities for how best to discover, access, or disrupt your systems, networks, and data. While any book on the topic will necessarily be incomplete, these chapters offer the fundamental building blocks that are both actionable today and equally applicable to future threats.

As with any foundational concepts, the cyber risk management techniques inherent to Embedded Endurance are intended to withstand the rapid evolution of the cyber landscape. While the threats may change along with the assets you protect, the fundamentals of Embedded Endurance will remain constant.

To illustrate this, we leave you with some cryptograms (distributed, secure, and informal messages over the blockchain) from the future. The cryptograms are sent to you from organizational leadership that needs your strategic cyber thinking. While these scenarios may not contain threats or assets ubiquitous today, you will notice that the core risk and risk mitigation concepts in this book that comprise an Embedded Endurance strategy will largely stand the test of time and apply to the questions posed.

Confronting Cyber Risk. Gregory Falco and Eric Rosenbach, Oxford University Press. © Oxford University Press 2022. DOI: 10.1093/oso/9780197526545.003.0009

Cryptogram 1

Wallet ID From: 13Dtw5cuqJV8CdmvE5enpzChfFV3L63YsN
Wallet ID To: 1EcJe1vop8JSrksgKwRhQvpQCa3dt69adr
Signature Verified: January 6, 2050 05:20:39 AM

I'm in a bind and could use your help. My company's been using autonomous drones for vaccine delivery in northeast Kenya, and we just found out the system's been hacked. Details are fuzzy, but it seems the attackers got into the commercial satellite network we rely on and spoofed the GPS systems of multiple drones with fake coordinates. This screwed up the drones' AI-based path optimization, so some have been delivering vaccines to nowhere.

It gets worse—as the infected drones spouted bad info, the data-driven AI mapping systems of uninfected drones also lost their grip on "ground truth." Some dropped their payloads in the wrong spots, while others wandered until the vaccines (which are temperature-sensitive) cooked in the sun.

So this is where we're at now. For a while the bad data slowed our attempts to track down the problem's root cause. Just last week we learned some drones had been reporting "mission success" for deliveries made to nowhere. Due to issues like this, our company's data for the past two months is poisoned. The question now is, how do we move forward from here? Who may have done this, and what was the motive? We need to be resilient to these scenarios in the future. This attack will cost us hundreds of thousands (millions when you toss in the lost productivity, reputation hit, and other liabilities).

Still, the worst part is we're not even the final victims here. Every drone gone awry means a handful of more unvaccinated people, and this disease isn't easing off the gas. Yesterday our lawyers pointed out the final toll of this thing will be measured in lives, not dollars.

You can see we're in over our heads. Any ideas on where we start?

Cryptogram 2

Wallet ID From: 17DKEzskXTB34sAgHGEnepRHfqyF4q3yE8
Wallet ID To: 1LtdsJsLdz1mCGo22Mewp97pUHTUVHywZ4
Signature Verified: August 8, 2050 02:16:07 AM

When our firm made an international push a few years back, we started using a highly regarded global provider of payment services. The company's dominance in China and its global reach made for a good fit with some of our overseas customer-facing platforms.

One of the major advantages of working with our payment processor is that they are at the forefront of quantum-encrypted communication. This is perfect for our payment services, which are full of sensitive information. When we signed up, they guaranteed that they would use their ultra-secure network of quantum comms satellites for transmitting payment data. While it's difficult to say anything is fully "hack-proof," the reality is that our provider's encryption is just about as close to unhackable as can be. And even if hackers do get in, the company can detect them almost instantly and lock down the breached comms lines in a matter of minutes.

So I was stunned last week when this "unhackable" company announced it had been hacked. I couldn't believe some cybercriminals could break our provider's quantum encryption, but it turns out they didn't have to. Their way in was much simpler: a basic (but well-coordinated) spear phishing attack on two of our provider's data management teams in Beijing and Berlin. The hackers followed the classic playbook—they gained credentials, escalated privileges, and then accessed troves of data on a poorly configured cloud server. While they didn't find a way to breach the quantum channels used for sending data, they found vulnerabilities at "home base," where it was stored.

Rumors are flying that the data of millions of customers was accessed, perhaps over several months. The potential systemic waves from a breach in a company as central as our payment processor are huge.

Right now we're in chaos mode. Are we liable if our customers' data was stolen? Given the international nature of our service provider, which jurisdiction of law is relevant? Could the hackers have compromising info about our own company's platforms and services that interface with the products our payment processor provides us?

What should we do preemptively to prepare for the worst here?

Cryptogram 3

Wallet ID From: 1PpkS7GTTh9HqptEATqvEE9MHTkrdMSpWp
Wallet ID To: 15qVK6NFJzCxUJqRJtPuTgs9PzwJBWiibr
Signature Verified: June 7, 2050 01:43:32 AM

Two months ago I started working for a market maker that deals primarily in energy securities. They've got a great setup: the pricing schemes are entirely data-driven, and everything is streamlined so that the data pipelines plug directly into the pricing algorithms. Granted, it's what most market makers do nowadays, but I'd been stuck at an old-fashioned firm previously, where they were still bogged down with more human involvement in the process.

Our system works like this. We have all sorts of data being piped in: geospatial imagery from satellites, weather reports, news-paper headlines that get digested by natural language processing algorithms, etc.—the whole nine yards. And then we set the bid-ask spread and provide the liquidity to make sure all goes smoothly.

Except it didn't go smoothly this week. We got hit with a cyberat-tack, a bad one—one that the computer folks here are calling a "state estimation attack." Basically, someone wormed their way into either the grid or our financial systems that pull supply/demand informa-tion from the grid. At this point it's not even clear whether it was the OT systems that were hacked or our IT systems.

A big issue is that the hackers were smart, and they only barely shifted the numbers, so the prices we were setting were only fractions of a cent off the price they should have been. But fractions of a cent add up over millions of trades. We don't know whether this has been going on for days or months, but the cost is going to be huge, not to mention the massive reputational hit that's in store. And given that we don't know if the issue is our systems or the raw incoming data, we don't know where to start.

Any idea what to do? Maybe we need to bring some more humans back in the loop to hedge the automation risk, but how do we make sure they don't become a new attack vector?

Notes

Chapter 1

1. Bossert, T. P. 2017. "It's Official: North Korea Is Behind WannaCry." *The Wall Street Journal.* December 18. https://www.wsj.com/articles/its-official-north-korea-is-behind-wannacry-1513642537.

2. Cameron, D. 2017. "Today's Massive Ransomware Attack Was Mostly Preventable; Here's How to Avoid It." Gizmodo. May 13. https://www.gizmodo.com.au/2017/05/todays-massive-ransomware-attack-was-mostly-preventable-heres-how-to-avoid-it/.

3. Jones, S., and T. Bradshaw. 2017. "Global Alert to Prepare for Fresh Cyber Attacks." *The Financial Times.* May 14. https://www.ft.com/content/bb4dda38-389f-11e7-821a-6027b8a20f23.

4. Whittaker, Z. 2019. "Marcus Hutchins, Malware Researcher and 'WannaCry Hero,' Sentenced to Supervised Release." TechCrunch. July 26. https://techcrunch.com/2019/07/26/marcus-hutchins-sentenced-kronos/.

5. Perlroth, N., and S. Shane. 2019. "In Baltimore and Beyond, a Stolen N.S.A. Tool Wreaks Havoc." *The New York Times.* May 25. https://www.nytimes.com/2019/05/25/us/nsa-hacking-tool-baltimore.html.

6. McMillan, R., J. Gross, and D. Roland. 2017. "Major Cyberattack Sweeps Globe, Hitting FedEx, U.K. Hospitals, Spanish Companies." *The Wall Street Journal.* May 12. https://www.wsj.com/articles/english-hospitals-hit-by-suspected-cyberattack-1494603884.

7. TSMC. 2018. "TSMC Details Impact of Computer Virus Incident." TSMC News Archives. August 5. https://pr.tsmc.com/english/news/1969.

8. CBC Newsroom. 2017. "Université de Montréal Computers Hit by Cyberattack Sweeping Globe." CBC News. May 15. https://www.cbc.ca/news/canada/montreal/universit%C3%A9-de-montr%C3%A9al-computers-hit-by-cyberattack-sweeping-globe-1.4116426.

9. Reuters Staff. 2017. "Honda Halts Japan Car Plant After WannaCry Virus Hits Computer Network." Reuters. June 21. https://www.reuters.com/article/us-honda-cyberattack/honda-halts-japan-car-plant-after-wannacry-virus-hits-computer-network-idUSKBN19C0EI.

10. Cyber Security Policy. 2018. "Securing Cyber Resilience in Health and Care: Progress Update October 2018." UK Department of Health & Social

Care. October. https://assets.publishing.service.gov.uk/government/uploads/ system/uploads/attachment_data/file/747464/securing-cyber-resilience-in-health-and-care-september-2018-update.pdf.

11. UK House of Commons Committee of Public Accounts. 2018. "Cyber-attack on the NHS: Thirty-Second Report of Session 2017–19." UK House of Commons. March 28. https://publications.parliament.uk/pa/cm201719/cmselect/cmpubacc/787/787.pdf.

12. Ibid.

13. NAO Comptroller and Auditor General. 2018. "Investigation: WannaCry Cyber Attack and the NHS." National Audit Office, UK Department of Health. April 25. https://www.nao.org.uk/wp-content/uploads/2017/10/Investigation-WannaCry-cyber-attack-and-the-NHS.pdf.

14. UK House of Commons Committee of Public Accounts. 2018. "Cyber-attack on the NHS: Thirty-Second Report of Session 2017–19." UK House of Commons. March 28. https://publications.parliament.uk/pa/cm201719/cmselect/cmpubacc/787/787.pdf.

15. Ibid.

16. Ibid.

17. Ibid.

18. NAO Comptroller and Auditor General. 2018. "Investigation: WannaCry Cyber Attack and the NHS." National Audit Office, UK Department of Health. April 25. https://www.nao.org.uk/wp-content/uploads/2017/10/Investigation-WannaCry-cyber-attack-and-the-NHS.pdf.

19. UK House of Commons Committee of Public Accounts. 2018. "Cyber-attack on the NHS: Thirty-Second Report of Session 2017–19." UK House of Commons. March 28. https://publications.parliament.uk/pa/cm201719/cmselect/cmpubacc/787/787.pdf.

20. Wells, D., B. Brewster, and B. Akhgar. 2016. "Challenges Priorities and Policies: Mapping the Research Requirements of Cybercrime and Cyberterrorism Stakeholders." In *Combating Cybercrime and Cyberterrorism: Challenges, Trends and Priorities*, B. Akhgar and B. Brewster, eds., 39–52. Sheffield: Springer International Publishing.

21. Antonucci, D. 2017. *The Cyber Risk Handbook: Creating and Measuring Effective Cybersecurity Capabilities*. Hoboken, NJ: John Wiley & Sons.

22. Ibid.

23. Denning, D. E. 2015. "Assessing Cyber War." In *Assessing War: The Challenge of Measuring Success and Failure*, L. J. Blanken., H. Rothstein, and J. J. Lepore, eds., 266–284. Washington, DC: Georgetown University Press.

24. Ibid.

25. Ibid.

26. Ibid.

27. Eccles, R. G., S. C. Newquist, and R. Schatz. 2007. "Reputation and Its Risks." *Harvard Business Review* 85, no. 2: 104.

28. National Institute of Standards and Technology. 2002. *Risk Management Guide for Information Technology System*. Special Publication 800-30. Washington, DC: NIST, p. 1.

29. Chaudhary, R., and J. Hamilton. 2015. "The Five Critical Attributes of Effective Cybersecurity Risk Management." Crowe Horwath. July. https://www.crowe.com/insights/asset/t/the-five-critical-attributes-of-effective-cybersecurity- risk-managemen

30. Falco, G., et al. 2019. "Cyber Risk Research Impeded by Disciplinary Barriers." *Science* 366, no. 6469: 1066–1069.

31. LeTellier, V. 2016. "The Argument for Holistic Cybersecurity." *Security.* June 28. https://www.securitymagazine.com/blogs/14-security-blog/post/87239-the-argument-for-holistic-cybersecurity [2017, November 2].

32. Chaudhary, R., and J. Hamilton. 2015. "The Five Critical Attributes of Effective Cybersecurity Risk Management." Crowe Horwath. July. https://www.crowe.com/insights/asset/t/the-five-critical-attributes-of-effective-cybersecurity-risk-managemen

33. Backofen, D. 2017. "Secure and Simple: Plug-and-Play Security." In *Cybersecurity. Simply. Make It Happen: Leveraging Digitization Through IT Security*, F. Abolhassan, ed., 87–100. Sheffield: Springer International Publishing.

34. Russell, B., and D. Van Duren. 2016. *Practical Internet of Things Security*. Birmingham: Packt Publishing.

35. Fortino, G., A. Guerrieri, W. Russo, and C. Savaglio. 2014. "Middlewares for Smart Objects and Smart Environments: Overview and Comparison." In *Internet of Things Based on Smart Objects: Technology, Middleware and Applications*, G. Fortino and P. Trunfio, eds., 1. New York: Springer International Publishing.

36. Russell, B., and D. Van Duren. 2016. *Practical Internet of Things Security*. Birmingham: Packt Publishing.

37. Gantz, S. D., and D. R. Philpott. 2012. *FISMA and the Risk Management Framework: The New Practice of Federal Cyber Security*. Waltham: Syngress.

38. Antonucci, D. 2017. *The Cyber Risk Handbook: Creating and Measuring Effective Cybersecurity Capabilities*. Hoboken, NJ: John Wiley & Sons.

39. Ponemon Institute. 2016. "The Second Annual Study on the Cyber Resilient Organization: Executive Summary." https://www.ibm.com/security/digital-assets/soar/cyber-resilient-organization-report/#/.

40. Antonucci, D. 2017. *The Cyber Risk Handbook: Creating and Measuring Effective Cybersecurity Capabilities*. Hoboken, NJ: John Wiley & Sons.

Chapter 2

1. Colonial Pipeline Company. 2021. "Frequently Asked Questions." Colonial Pipeline: About Us. May 20. https://www.colpipe.com/about-us/faqs.
2. Eaton, Collin, and Dustin Volz. 2021. "Colonial Pipeline CEO Tells Why He Paid Hackers a $4.4 Million Ransom." *The Wall Street Journal.* May 19. https://www.wsj.com/articles/colonial-pipeline-ceo-tells-why-he-paid-hackers-a-4-4-million-ransom-11621435636.
3. Colonial Pipeline Company. 2021. "Media Statement Update: Colonial Pipeline System Disruption." Press release. May 8. https://www.colpipe.com/news/press-releases/media-statement-colonial-pipeline-system-disruption.
4. Eaton, Collin, and Dustin Volz. 2021. "Colonial Pipeline CEO Tells Why He Paid Hackers a $4.4 Million Ransom." *The Wall Street Journal.* May 19. https://www.wsj.com/articles/colonial-pipeline-ceo-tells-why-he-paid-hackers-a-4-4-million-ransom-11621435636.
5. Robertson, Jordan, and William Turton. 2021. "Colonial Hackers Stole Data Thursday Ahead of Shutdown." Bloomberg. May 8. https://www.bloomberg.com/news/articles/2021-05-09/colonial-hackers-stole-data-thursday-ahead-of-pipeline-shutdown?sref=SCAzRb9t.
6. Englund, Will, and Ellen Nakashima. 2021. "Panic Buying Strikes Southeastern United States as Shuttered Pipeline Resumes Operations." *The Washington Post.* May 12..
7. Rosa-Aquino, Paola, and Chas Danner. 2021. "What We Know About the Colonial Pipeline Shutdown." *New York Magazine.* May 16. https://nymag.com/intelligencer/article/what-we-know-about-the-colonial-pipeline-shutdown-updates.html.
8. Newman, Lily Hay. 2021. "Colonial Pipeline Paid a $5M Ransom—and Kept a Vicious Cycle Turning." *Wired.* May 14. https://www.wired.com/story/colonial-pipeline-ransomware-payment/.
9. Falco, Gregory, Alicia Noriega, and Lawrence Susskind. 2019. "Cyber Negotiation: A Cyber Risk Management Approach to Defend Urban Critical Infrastructure from Cyberattacks." *Journal of Cyber Policy* 4, no. 1: 90–116.
10. Eaton, Collin, and Dustin Volz. 2021. "Colonial Pipeline CEO Tells Why He Paid Hackers a $4.4 Million Ransom." *The Wall Street Journal.* May 19. https://www.wsj.com/articles/colonial-pipeline-ceo-tells-why-he-paid-hackers-a-4-4-million-ransom-11621435636.
11. Colonial Pipeline Company. 2021. "Frequently Asked Questions." Colonial Pipeline: About Us. May 20. https://www.colpipe.com/about-us/faqs.
12. Ibid.
13. Colonial Pipeline Company. 2021. "Media Statement Update: Colonial Pipeline System Disruption." Press release. May 8. https://www.colpipe.com/news/press-releases/media-statement-colonial-pipeline-system-disruption.

14. Eaton, Collin, and Dustin Volz. 2021. "Colonial Pipeline CEO Tells Why He Paid Hackers a $4.4 Million Ransom." *The Wall Street Journal.* May 19. https://www.wsj.com/articles/colonial-pipeline-ceo-tells-why-he-paid-hackers-a-4-4-million-ransom-11621435636.

15. Englund, Will, and Ellen Nakashima. 2021. "Panic Buying Strikes Southeastern United States as Shuttered Pipeline Resumes Operations." *The Washington Post.* May 12. https://www.washingtonpost.com/business/2021/05/12/gas-shortage-colonial-pipeline-live-updates/.

16. Knutson, Jacob. 2021. "Gas Shortages Persist After Colonial Pipeline Restarts Service." Axios. May 14. https://www.axios.com/gas-shortage-colonial-pipeline-restarts-265c488d-ff19-4ae8-b020-f9aa80db665a.html.

17. Rosa-Aquino, Paola, and Chas Danner. 2021. "What We Know About the Colonial Pipeline Shutdown." *New York Magazine.* May 16. https://nymag.com/intelligencer/article/what-we-know-about-the-colonial-pipeline-shutdown-updates.html.

18. Eaton, Collin, and Dustin Volz. 2021. "Colonial Pipeline CEO Tells Why He Paid Hackers a $4.4 Million Ransom." *The Wall Street Journal.* May 19. https://www.wsj.com/articles/colonial-pipeline-ceo-tells-why-he-paid-hackers-a-4-4-million-ransom-11621435636.

19. FBI National Press Office. 2021. "FBI Statement on Compromise of Colonial Pipeline Networks." Federal Bureau of Investigation (FBI) News. May 10. https://www.fbi.gov/news/pressrel/press-releases/fbi-statement-on-compromise-of-colonial-pipeline-networks.

20. Volz, Dustin, Robert McMillan, and Collin Eaton. 2021. "Colonial Pipeline Said to Pay Ransom to Hackers Who Caused Shutdown." *The Wall Street Journal.* May 13. https://www.wsj.com/articles/colonial-pipeline-expects-to-fully-restore-service-thursday-following-cyberattack-11620917499.

21. McMillan, Robert, and Dustin Volz. 2021. "Colonial Pipeline Hacker DarkSide Says It Will Shut Operations." *The Wall Street Journal.* May 14. https://www.wsj.com/articles/web-site-of-darkside-hacking-group-linked-to-colonial-pipeline-attack-is-down-11621001688.

22. Nuce, Jordan, Jeremy Kennelly, Kimberly Goody, Andrew Moore, Alyssa Rahman, Matt Williams, Brendan McKeague, and Jared Wilson. 2021. "Shining a Light on DARKSIDE Ransomware Operations." FireEye Threat Research. May 11. https://www.fireeye.com/blog/threat-research/2021/05/shining-a-light-on-darkside-ransomware-operations.html.

23. McMillan, Robert, and Dustin Volz. 2021. "Colonial Pipeline Hacker DarkSide Says It Will Shut Operations." *The Wall Street Journal.* May 14. https://www.wsj.com/articles/web-site-of-darkside-hacking-group-linked-to-colonial-pipeline-attack-is-down-11621001688.

24. Budington, Bill. 2021. "FAQ: DarkSide Ransomware Group and Colonial Pipeline." Electronic Frontier Foundation. May 13. https://www.eff.org/deeplinks/2021/05/faq-darkside-ransomware-group-and-colonial-pipeline.

25. Dissent. 2021. "'We Are Apolitical'—DarkSide Threat Actors." DataBreaches. May 10. https://www.databreaches.net/we-are-apolitical-darkside-threat-actors.

26. Nuce, Jordan, Jeremy Kennelly, Kimberly Goody, Andrew Moore, Alyssa Rahman, Matt Williams, Brendan McKeague, and Jared Wilson. 2021. "Shining a Light on DARKSIDE Ransomware Operations." FireEye Threat Research. May 11. https://www.fireeye.com/blog/threat-research/2021/05/shining-a-light-on-darkside-ransomware-operations.html.

27. George, Torsten. 2017. "Cyber Risk, Cyber Threats, and Cyber Security: Synonyms or Oxymorons?" *Security Week.* March 15. http://www.securityweek.com/cyber-risk-cyber-threats-and-cyber-security-synonyms-or-oxymorons.

28. RSA Security LLC. 2016. "Cyber Risk Appetite: Defining and Understanding Risk in the Modern Enterprise." RSA White Paper. https://community.rsa.com/yfcdo34327/attachments/yfcdo34327/archer-blog/2108/1/cyber-risk-appetite-wp.pdf.

29. Ibid.

30. Ibid.

31. Paganini, Pierluigi. 2017. "The Most Common Social Engineering Attacks." Infosec. http://resources.infosecinstitute.com/common-social-engineering-attacks/.

32. Ibid.

33. Ibid.

34. Ibid.

35. Eykholt, K., et al. 2018. "Robust Physical-World Attacks on Deep Learning Visual Classification." In *Proceedings of the IEEE Conference on Computer Vision and Pattern Recognition,* 1625–1634.

36. Fowler, K. 2016. *Data Breach Preparation and Response: Breaches Are Certain, Impact Is Not.* Cambridge: Syngress, 15–18.

37. Edgar, T. W., and D. O. Manz. 2017. *Research Methods for Cybersecurity.* Cambridge: Syngress, 39.

38. BAE Systems. 2016. "The Unusual Suspects: Cyber Threats, Methods, and Motivations." http://www.baesystems.com/en/cybersecurity/feature/the-unusual-suspects.

39. Ibid.

40. Fowler, K. 2016. *Data Breach Preparation and Response: Breaches Are Certain, Impact Is Not.* Cambridge: Syngress, 9.

41. Ibid., 7.

42. Donaldson, S. E., S. G. Siegel, C. K. Williams, and A. Aslam. 2015. *Enterprise Cybersecurity: How to Build a Successful Cyberdefense Program Against Advanced Threats.* New York: Springer Science + Business Media, 7.

43. Hill, J. B., and N. E. Marion. 2016. *Introduction to Cybercrime: Computer Crimes, Laws and Policing in the 21st Century.* California: ABC-CLIO, 136.

44. Fowler, K. 2016. *Data Breach Preparation and Response: Breaches Are Certain, Impact Is Not.* Cambridge: Syngress. 18.

45. Ibid.

46. Hewlett Packard. 2016. "Countering Nation State Cyber Threats." http://files.asset.microfocus.com/4aa6-6901/en/4aa6-6901.pdf.

47. Ibid.

48. Fowler, K. 2016. *Data Breach Preparation and Response: Breaches Are Certain, Impact Is Not.* Cambridge: Syngress, 11.

49. Gisclair, J. 2008. "The Dissonance Between Culture and Intellectual Property in China." *Southeast Review of Asian Studies* 30:182–187.

50. Allison, G. 2017. "What Xi Jinping Wants." *The Atlantic.* May 31. https://www.theatlantic.com/international/archive/2017/05/what-china-wants/528561/.

51. Brown, G., and C. D. Yung. 2017. "Evaluating the US-China Cybersecurity Agreement, Part 2: China's Take on Cyberspace and Cybersecurity." *The Diplomat.* January 19. https://thediplomat.com/2017/01/evaluating-the-us-china-cybersecurity-agreement-part-2-chinas-take-on-cyberspace-and-cybersecurity/.

52. Sanger, David E., Nicole Perlroth, Glenn Thrush, and Alan Rappeport. 2018. "Marriott Data Breach Is Traced to Chinese Hackers as U.S. Readies Crackdown on Beijing." *The New York Times.* December 11. https://www.nytimes.com/2018/12/11/us/politics/trump-china-trade.html.

53. Fisher, M. 2016. "In D.N.C. Hack, Echoes of Russia's New Approach to Power." *The New York Times.* July 26. https://www.nytimes.com/2016/07/26/world/europe/russia-dnc-putin-strategy.html?_r=0.

54. Jun, J., S. LaFoy, and E. Sohn. 2015. "North Korea's Cyber Operations: Strategy and Responses." Center for Strategic and International Studies. December. http://csis-website-prod.s3.amazonaws.com/s3fs-public/legacy_files/files/publication/151216_Cha_NorthKoreasCyberOperations_Web.pdf, 5.

55. Edwards, W. 2016. "North Korea as a Cyber Threat." The Cipher Brief. July 1. https://www.thecipherbrief.com/article/asia/north-korea-as-a-cyber-threat.

56. Sanger, David E., and Nicole Perlroth. 2020. "U.S. Accuses North Korea of Cyberattacks, a Sign That Deterrence Is Failing." *The New York Times.* Last updated April 26. https://www.nytimes.com/2020/04/15/world/asia/north-korea-cyber.html.

57. Eisenstadt, M. 2016. "Iran's Lengthening Cyber Shadow." Washington Institute. Policy Analysis Research Note 34. July 28. https://www.washingtoninstitute.org/policy-analysis/irans-lengthening-cyber-shadow.

58. Ibid.

59. World Economic Forum. 2016. "Understanding Systemic Cyber Risk." White paper. https://www.weforum.org/whitepapers/understanding-systemic-cyber-risk, 9.

60. Ibid.
61. Marsh & McLennan Companies. 2016. "MMC Cyber Handbook 2016: Increasing Resilience in the Digital Economy." https://www.mmc.com/content/dam/mmc-web/Global-Risk-Center/Files/MMC-Cyber-Handbook_2016-web-final.pdf.
62. Deloitte. 2016. "Cyber Risk in Advanced Manufacturing." https://www2.deloitte.com/us/en/pages/manufacturing/articles/cyber-risk-in-advanced-manufacturing.html.
63. Marsh & McLennan Companies. 2016. "MMC Cyber Handbook 2016: Increasing Resilience in the Digital Economy." https://www.mmc.com/content/dam/mmc-web/Global-Risk-Center/Files/MMC-Cyber-Handbook_2016-web-final.pdf.
64. Deloitte. 2016. "Cyber Risk in Advanced Manufacturing." https://www2.deloitte.com/us/en/pages/manufacturing/articles/cyber-risk-in-advanced-manufacturing.html.
65. Raman, A., F. Kabir, S. Hejazi, and K. Aggarwal. 2016. "Cybersecurity in Higher Education: The Changing Threat Landscape." *Performance* 8, no. 3:46–53.
66. Ibid.
67. Campbell, Richard J. 2015. "Cybersecurity Issues for the Bulk Power System." Congressional Research Service. June 10. https://fas.org/sgp/crs/misc/R43989.pdf.
68. Ibid.
69. Ankeny, Jason. 2017. "3 Trends Shaping Retail Cybersecurity in 2017." Retail Dive. February 13. http://www.retaildive.com/news/3-trends-shaping-retail-cybersecurity-in-2017/435868/.
70. Falco, Gregory. 2018. "Cybersecurity Principles for Space Systems." *Journal of Aerospace Information Systems* 16, no. 2. https://arc.aiaa.org/doi/abs/10.2514/1.I010693?journalCode=jais.

Chapter 3

1. Cerulus, Laurens. 2019. "How Ukraine Became a Test Bed for Cyberweaponry." Politico. February 14. https://www.politico.eu/article/ukraine-cyber-war-frontline-russia-malware-attacks/.
2. National Cybersecurity and Communications Integration Center. 2016. "NCCIC/ICS-CERT Incident Alert: Cyber-Attack Against Ukraining Critical Infrastructure." U.S. Department of Homeland Security. March 7. https://info.publicintelligence.net/NCCIC-UkrainianPowerAttack.pdf.
3. Ibid.
4. Sobczak, Blake, and Peter Behr. 2016. "Inside the Ukrainian Hack That put U.S. Grid on High Alert." E&E News. July 18. https://www.eenews.net/stories/1060040399/.

5. Styczynski, Jake, and Nate Beach-Westmoreland. 2019. "When the Lights Went Out: A Comprehensive Review of the 2015 Attacks on Ukrainian Critical Infrastructure." Booz Allen Hamilton. https://www.boozallen.com/content/dam/boozallen/documents/2016/09/ukraine-report-when-the-lights-went-out.pdf.

6. Pagliery, Jose. 2016. "Scary Questions in Ukraine Energy Grid Hack." CNN. January 18. https://money.cnn.com/2016/01/18/technology/ukraine-hack-russia/.

7. Styczynski, Jake, and Nate Beach-Westmoreland. 2019. "When the Lights Went Out: A Comprehensive Review of the 2015 Attacks on Ukrainian Critical Infrastructure." Booz Allen Hamilton. https://www.boozallen.com/content/dam/boozallen/documents/2016/09/ukraine-report-when-the-lights-went-out.pdf.

8. National Cybersecurity and Communications Integration Center. 2016. "NCCIC/ICS-CERT Incident Alert: Cyber-Attack Against Ukraining Critical Infrastructure." U.S. Department of Homeland Security. March 7. https://info.publicintelligence.net/NCCIC-UkrainianPowerAttack.pdf.

9. Zetter, Kim. 2016. "Inside the Cunning, Unprecedented Hack of Ukraine's Power Grid." Wired. March 3. https://www.wired.com/2016/03/inside-cunning-unprecedented-hack-ukraines-power-grid/.

10. National Cybersecurity and Communications Integration Center. 2016. "NCCIC/ICS-CERT Incident Alert: Cyber-Attack Against Ukraining Critical Infrastructure." U.S. Department of Homeland Security. March 7. https://info.publicintelligence.net/NCCIC-UkrainianPowerAttack.pdf.

11. Styczynski, Jake, and Nate Beach-Westmoreland. 2019. "When the Lights Went Out: A Comprehensive Review of the 2015 Attacks on Ukrainian Critical Infrastructure." Booz Allen Hamilton. https://www.boozallen.com/content/dam/boozallen/documents/2016/09/ukraine-report-when-the-lights-went-out.pdf.

12. Behr, Peter, and Blake Sobczak. 2016. "Utilities Look Back to the Future for Hands-On Cyberdefense." The Hack. July 21. https://www.eenews.net/special_reports/the_hack/stories/1060040590.

13. Ibid.

14. Sobczak, Blake, and Peter Behr. 2016. "Inside the Ukrainian Hack That Put U.S. Grid on High Alert." E&E News. July 18. https://www.eenews.net/stories/1060040399/.

15. Zetter, Kim. 2016. "Inside the Cunning, Unprecedented Hack of Ukraine's Power Grid." Wired. March 3. https://www.wired.com/2016/03/inside-cunning-unprecedented-hack-ukraines-power-grid/.

16. National Cybersecurity and Communications Integration Center. 2016. "NCCIC/ICS-CERT Incident Alert: Cyber-Attack Against Ukraining Critical Infrastructure." U.S. Department of Homeland Security. March 7. https://info.publicintelligence.net/NCCIC-UkrainianPowerAttack.pdf.

17. Sobczak, Blake, and Peter Behr. 2016. "Inside the Ukrainian Hack That Put U.S. Grid on High Alert." E&E News. July 18. https://www.eenews.net/stories/1060040399/.

18. Ibid.

19. Behr, Peter, and Blake Sobczak. 2016. "Grid Hack Exposes Troubling Security Gaps for Local Utilities." The Hack. July 20. https://www.eenews.net/special_reports/the_hack/stories/1060040519.

20. National Cybersecurity and Communications Integration Center. 2016. "NCCIC/ICS-CERT Incident Alert: Cyber-Attack Against Ukraining Critical Infrastructure." U.S. Department of Homeland Security. March 7. https://info.publicintelligence.net/NCCIC-UkrainianPowerAttack.pdf.

21. Sobczak, Blake, and Peter Behr. 2016. "Inside the Ukrainian Hack That Put U.S. Grid on High Alert." E&E News. July 18. https://www.eenews.net/stories/1060040399/.

22. National Cybersecurity and Communications Integration Center. 2016. "NCCIC/ICS-CERT Incident Alert: Cyber-Attack Against Ukraining Critical Infrastructure." U.S. Department of Homeland Security. March 7. https://info.publicintelligence.net/NCCIC-UkrainianPowerAttack.pdf.

23. Singer, P. W., and A. Friedman. 2014. Cybersecurity and Cyberwar: What Everyone Needs to Know. New York: Oxford University Press.

24. Ibid.

25. Filkins, B. 2017. "Network Security Infrastructure and Best Practices: A SANS Survey." https://www.sans.org/webcasts/network-security-infrastructure-practices-survey-104097/.

26. Ibid.

27. Rouse, M. 2014. "Confidentiality, Integrity, and Availability (CIA Triad)." Tech Target. http://whatis.techtarget.com/definition/Confidentiality-integrity-and-availability-CIA.

28. Swanson, M., P. Bowen, A. W. Phillips, D. Gallup, and D. Lynes. 2010. "Contingency Planning Guide for Federal Information Systems." http://nvlpubs.nist.gov/nistpubs/Legacy/SP/nistspecialpublication800-34r1.pdf.

29. Mohammad bin Salman is currently the crown prince and minister of defense of Saudi Arabia.

Chapter 4

1. Gordon v. Nielsen et al. 2018. "Complaint for Violation of the Federal Securities Laws." U.S. District Court, Southern District of New York. August 8. https://www.docketbird.com/court-documents/Gordon-v-Nielsen-Holdings-PLC-et-al/COMPLAINT-against-Dwight-Mitchell-Barns-Jamere-Jackson-Nielsen-Holdings-PLC-Filing-Fee-400-00-Receipt-Number-0208-15425974-Document-filed-by-Craig-Gordon/nysd-1:2018-cv-07143-0.

2. Cattanach, Robert E., and Sam Bolstad. 2018. "Sued for Misjudging the Impact of GDPR and Other Changes to the Consumer Data Privacy Landscape—Yes That Just Happened." TMCA. August 30. https://thetmca.com/sued-for-misjudging-the-impact-of-gdpr-and-other-changes-to-the-consumer-data-privacy-landscape-yes-that-just-happened/.

3. Mooney, Joshua, and Andrew Lipton. 2018. "Corporate Statements About GDPR Spark Securities Class Action Lawsuit." White and Williams, LLP. September 6. https://www.whiteandwilliams.com/resources-alerts-Corporate_Satements_About_GDPR_Spark_Securities_Class_Action_Lawsuit.html.

4. Gordon v. Nielsen et al. 2018. "Complaint for Violation of the Federal Securities Laws." U.S. District Court, Southern District of New York. August 8. https://www.docketbird.com/court-documents/Gordon-v-Nielsen-Holdings-PLC-et-al/COMPLAINT-against-Dwight-Mitchell-Barns-Jamere-Jackson-Nielsen-Holdings-PLC-Filing-Fee-400-00-Receipt-Number-0208-15425974-Document-filed-by-Craig-Gordon/nysd-1:2018-cv-07143-0.

5. Ibid.

6. Business Wire. 2018. "Robbins Geller Rudman & Dowd LLP Files Class Action Suit Against Nielsen Holdings PLC." August 8. https://www.businesswire.com/news/home/20180808005871/en/Robbins-Geller-Rudman-Dowd-LLP-Files-Class.

7. Bhattacharya v. Nielsen Holdings PLC et al. 2018. "Bhattacharya v. Nielsen Holdings PLC et al. Court Docket Sheet." U.S. Southern District of New York. October 17. https://www.docketbird.com/court-cases/Bhattacharya-v-Nielsen-Holdings-PLC-et-al/nysd-1:2018-cv-07677.

8. Gordon v. Nielsen et al. 2018. "Complaint for Violation of the Federal Securities Laws." U.S. District Court, Southern District of New York. August 8. https://www.docketbird.com/court-documents/Gordon-v-Nielsen-Holdings-PLC-et-al/COMPLAINT-against-Dwight-Mitchell-Barns-Jamere-Jackson-Nielsen-Holdings-PLC-Filing-Fee-400-00-Receipt-Number-0208-15425974-Document-filed-by-Craig-Gordon/nysd-1:2018-cv-07143-0.

9. Ibid.

10. Bhattacharya v. Nielsen Holdings PLC et al. 2018. "Bhattacharya v. Nielsen Holdings PLC et al. Court Docket Sheet." U.S. Southern District of New York. October 17. https://www.docketbird.com/court-cases/Bhattacharya-v-Nielsen-Holdings-PLC-et-al/nysd-1:2018-cv-07677.

11. Ibid.

12. Ibid.

13. Gordon v. Nielsen et al. 2018. "Complaint for Violation of the Federal Securities Laws." U.S. District Court, Southern District of New York. August 8. https://www.docketbird.com/court-documents/Gordon-v-Nielsen-Holdings-PLC-et-al/COMPLAINT-against-Dwight-Mitchell-Barns-Jamere-Jackson-Nielsen-Holdings-PLC-Filing-Fee-400-00-Receipt-Number-0208-15425974-Document-filed-by-Craig-Gordon/nysd-1:2018-cv-07143-0.

14. Kramer, Alexis. 2019. "Securities Fraud Claims Get Boost from EU Data Privacy Rules." Bloomberg Law. February 1.

15. LaCroix, Kevin. 2018. "Investors Filed GDPR-Related Securities Suit Against Nielsen Holdings." The D&O Diary. August 27. https://www.dandodiary.com/2018/08/articles/securities-litigation/investors-filed-gdpr-related-securities-suit-nielsen-holdings/.

16. Kramer, Alexis. 2019. "Securities Fraud Claims Get Boost from EU Data Privacy Rules." Bloomberg Law. February 1. https://news.bloomberglaw.com/tech-and-telecom-law/securities-fraud-claims-get-boost-from-eu-data-privacy-rules.

17. Ibid.

18. Cattanach, Robert E., and Sam Bolstad. 2018. "Sued for Misjudging the Impact of GDPR and Other Changes to the Consumer Data Privacy Landscape—Yes That Just Happened." TMCA. August 30. https://thetmca.com/sued-for-misjudging-the-impact-of-gdpr-and-other-changes-to-the-consumer-data-privacy-landscape-yes-that-just-happened/.

19. Hagermann, K. 2016. "Security vs. Compliance." Armor. https://www.armor.com/blog/security-vs-compliance/.

20. Ilan, D., and K. M. Carroll. 2017. "NYDFS Cybersecurity Regulations Take Effect." Harvard Law School Forum on Corporate Governance and Financial Regulation. September 2. https://corpgov.law.harvard.edu/2017/09/02/nydfs-cybersecurity-regulations-take-effect/.

21. Fischer, E. A. 2014. "Federal Laws Relating to Cybersecurity: Overview of Major Issues, Current Laws, and Proposed Legislation." Federation of American Scientists. https://fas.org/sgp/crs/natsec/.

22. U.S. Department of Health and Human Services. 2013. "Summary of HIPAA Privacy Rule." https://www.hhs.gov/hipaa/for-professionals/privacy/laws-regulations/index.html.

23. Federal Trade Commission. n.d. "Gramm-Leach-Bliley Act." https://www.ftc.gov/tips-advice/business-center/privacy-and-security/gramm-leach-bliley-act.

24. Lord, N. 2017. "What Is FISMA Compliance?" Digital Guardian. https://digitalguardian.com/blog/what-fisma-compliance-fisma-definition-requirements-penalties-and-more.

25. Deloitte. 2013. "FISMA Takes Private Sector by Surprise." http://deloitte.wsj.com/cio/2013/06/03/fisma-takes-private-sector-by-surprise/.

26. Salomon, S. 2016. "Are You Confident That Your Organization Is FISMA Compliant?" IS Partners LLC. https://www.ispartnersllc.com/blog/confident-organization-fisma-compliant/.

27. Lord, N. 2017. "What Is FISMA Compliance? FISMA Definition, Requirements, Penalties, and More." Digital Guardian. https://digitalguardian.com/blog/what-fisma-compliance-fisma-definition-requirements-penalties-and-more.

28. Nadeau, M. 2017. "General Data Protection Regulation (GDPR) Requirements, Deadlines and Facts." CSO. https://www.csoonline.com/article/3202771/data-protection/general-data-protection-regulation-gdpr-requirements-deadlines-and-facts.html.

29. SecureDataService. 2017. "Article 4 EU GDPR 'Definitions.'" http://www.privacy-regulation.eu/en/article-4-definitions-GDPR.htm.

30. Ibid.

31. Intersoft Consulting. n.d. "Art. 12 GDPR: Transparent Information, Communication and Modalities for the Exercise of the Rights of the Data Subject." https://gdpr-info.eu/art-12-gdpr/.

32. Intersoft Consulting. n.d. "Art. 33 GDPR: Notification of a Personal Data Breach to the Supervisory Authority." https://gdpr-info.eu/art-33-gdpr/.

33. O'Neill, C. 2017. "GDPR Series, Part 4: The Penalties for Non-Compliance." Imperva. https://www.imperva.com/blog/2017/03/gdpr-series-part-4-penalties-non-compliance/.

34. Division of Corporate Finance, U.S. Securities and Exchange Commission. 2011. "CF Disclosure Guidance: Topic No. 2." https://www.sec.gov/divisions/corpfin/guidance/cfguidance-topic2.htm.

35. U.S. Securities and Exchange Commission. 2014. "SEC Charges Lions Gate with Disclosure Failures While Preventing Hostile Takeover." March 13. https://www.sec.gov/news/press-release/2014-51.

36. Peacock, Justin. 2019. "What Is NERC CIP." CyberSaint Security. https://www.cybersaint.io/blog/what-is-nerc-cip.

37. North American Electric Reliability Corporation. 2019. "CIP Standards." NERC Standards. https://www.nerc.com/pa/Stand/Pages/CIPStandards.aspx.

38. Michalsons. 2014. "PCI DSS Compliance." https://www.michalsons.com/blog/pci-dss-compliance/46; PCI DSS Compliance. n.d. "Fines for Non-Compliance." http://pcidsscompliance.net/overview/fines-for-non-compliance/.

39. InfoLawGroup. 2010. "FAQ on Washington State's PCI Law." https://www.infolawgroup.com/2010/03/articles/payment-card-breach-laws/faq-on-washington-states-pci-law/; Rosenfeld, D., and C. Loeffler. 2010. "Washington State Enacts PCI Bill." Kelley Drye. March 25. https://www.kelleydrye.com/News-Events/Publications/Client-Advisories/Washington-State-Enacts-PCI-Bill.

40. Antonucci, D. 2017. *The Cyber Risk Handbook: Creating and Measuring Effective Cybersecurity Capabilities*. New York: John Wiley and Sons.

41. Chaudhary, R., and J. Hamilton. 2015. "The Five Critical Attributes of Effective Cybersecurity Risk Management." Crowe Horwath. July. https://icscsi.org/library/Documents/Risk_Management/Crowe%20Horwath%20-%205%20Critical%20Attributes%20of%20Effective%20Cybersecurity%20Risk%20Management.pdf.

42. Ferrillo, P. 2014. "Cyber Security, Cyber Governance, and Cyber Insurance." Harvard Law School Forum on Corporate Governance. November 13. https://corpgov.law.harvard.edu/2014/11/13/cyber-security-cyber-governance-and-cyber-insurance/.

43. Rybaltowski, M. 2015. "How to Find the Best Cyber Security Insurance for Your Firm." Reuters. June 26. http://www.reuters.com/article/us-advisers-insurance-cybersecurity/how-to-find-the-best-cyber-security-insurance-for-your-firm-idUSKBN0P61V520150626.

44. Falco, G., et al. 2021. "Cyber Crossroads: A Global Research Collaborative on Cyber Risk Governance." S&P Global Ratings Cyber Crossroads Launch. May 25, 2021. https://cybercrossroads.org.

Chapter 5

1. Smith, Richard F. 2017. "Prepared Testimony of Richard F. Smith Before the U.S. House Committee on Energy and Commerce Subcommittee on Digital Commerce and Consumer Protection." U.S. House of Representatives Meeting Archives. October 3. https://docs.house.gov/meetings/IF/IF17/20171003/106455/HHRG-115-IF17-Wstate-SmithR-20171003.pdf.

2. Schneier, Bruce. 2017. "Testimony and Statement for the Record of Bruce Schneier Before the Subcommittee on Digital Commerce and Consumer Protection." Schneier on Security. November 1. https://www.schneier.com/blog/archives/2017/11/me_on_the_equif.html; U.S. House of Representatives Committee on Oversight and Government Reform. 2018. "The Equifax Data Breach." Committee on Oversight and Government Reform Archives. December. https://republicans-oversight.house.gov/wp-content/uploads/2018/12/Equifax-Report.pdf.

3. Equifax. 2017. "Equifax's Statement for the Record Regarding the Extent of the Cybersecurity Incident Announced on September 7, 2017." SEC Archives. https://www.sec.gov/Archives/edgar/data/33185/000119312518154706/d583804dex991.htm.

4. Ibid.

5. Whittaker, Zack. 2018. "Equifax Breach Was 'Entirely Preventable' Had It Used Basic Security Measures, Says House Report." TechCrunch. December 10. https://techcrunch.com/2018/12/10/equifax-breach-preventable-house-oversight-report/.

6. FTC Press Office. 2019. "Equifax to Pay $575 Million as Part of Settlement with FTC, CFPB, and States Related to 2017 Data Breach." U.S. Federal Trade Commission. July 22. https://www.ftc.gov/news-events/press-releases/2019/07/equifax-pay-575-million-part-settlement-ftc-cfpb-states-related.

7. U.S. House of Representatives Committee on Oversight and Government Reform. 2018. "The Equifax Data Breach." Committee on Oversight and Government Reform Archives. December. https://republicans-oversight.house.gov/wp-content/uploads/2018/12/Equifax-Report.pdf.

8. Ibid.

9. Ibid.

10. Ibid.

11. Larson, Selena. 2017. "Every Single Yahoo Account Was Hacked—3 Billion in All." CNN. October 4. https://money.cnn.com/2017/10/03/technology/business/yahoo-breach-3-billion-accounts/index.html.

12. Perlroth, Nicole. 2017. "All 3 Billion Yahoo Accounts Were Affected by 2013 Attack." *The New York Times*. October 3. https://www.nytimes.com/2017/10/03/technology/yahoo-hack-3-billion-users.html.

13. World Economic Forum. 2017. "Advancing Cyber Resilience: Principles and Tools for Boards." http://www3.weforum.org/docs/IP/2017/Adv_Cyber_Resilience_Principles-Tools.pdf.

14. Mattord, H., and M. Whitman. 2016. *Management of Information Security*. 5th ed. Boston: Cengage Learning, 26–28, 45, 145–148.

15. Ibid.

16. Lambarque, K. 2017. "Former Equifax CEO Blames Breach on One IT Employee." Engadget. October 3. https://www.engadget.com/2017/10/03/former-equifax-ceo-blames-breach-on-one-it-employee/.

17. Falco, G., et al. 2021. "Governing AI Safety Through Independent Audits." *Nature Machine Intelligence* 3:566–571.

18. Hindawi, O., and L. Modano. 2016. "Bridging the Accountability Gap: Why We Need to Adopt a Culture of Responsibility." NASDAQ. http://business.nasdaq.com/marketinsite/2016/Bridging-the-Accountability-Gap-Why-We-Need-to-Adopt-a-Culture-of-Responsibility.html.

19. Ibid.

20. Ibid.

21. Centre for Cyber Security Belgium. 2016. "Cyber Security Incident Management Guide." https://www.cybersecuritycoalition.be/content/uploads/cybersecurity-incident-management-guide-EN.pdf.

22. Deloitte and National Association of State Chief Information Officers (NASCIO). 2016. "2016 Deloitte-NASCIO Cybersecurity Study: State Governments at Risk: Turning Strategy and Awareness into Progress." https://dupress.deloitte.com/content/dam/dup-us-en/articles/3470_2016-Deloitte-NASCIO-cybersecurity-study/2016-Deloitte-NASCIO-Cybersecurity-Study.pdf.

23. Ferran, L. 2013. "Report Fingers Chinese Military Unit in US Hack Attacks." ABC News. February 19. http://abcnews.go.com/Blotter/mandiant-report-fingers-chinese-military-us-hack-attacks/story?id=18537307.

24. National Institute of Standards and Technology. 2008. "Performance Measurement Guide for Information Security." NIST Special Publication 800-55 Revision 1. http://nvlpubs.nist.gov/nistpubs/Legacy/SP/nistspecialpublication 800-55r1.pdf.

25. Ibid.

26. Ibid.

27. Ibid.

28. Ibid.

29. Ibid.

30. Oltsik, J. 2016. "The State of Cyber Security Professional Careers, Part 1." ESG/ISSA. October. http://www.esg-global.com/hubfs/issa/ESG-ISSA-Research-Report-State-of-Cybersecurity-Professional-Careers-Oct-2016.pdf.

31. Winnefeld, James A. Jr., Christopher Kirchhoff, and David M. Upton. 2015. "Cybersecurity's Human Factor: Lessons from the Pentagon." *Harvard Business Review*. September. https://hbr.org/2015/09/cybersecuritys-human-factor-lessons-from-the-pentagon.

Chapter 6

1. Sanger, David E., Nicole Perlroth, and Julian E. Barnes. 2021. "As Understanding of Russian Hacking Grows, So Does Alarm." *The New York Times*. January 2. https://www.nytimes.com/2021/01/02/us/politics/russian-hacking-government.html.

2. Strobel, Warren P. 2020. "Pompeo Blames Russia for Hack as Trump Casts Doubt on Widespread Conclusion." *The Wall Street Journal*. December 19. https://www.wsj.com/articles/pompeo-blames-russia-for-solarwinds-hack-11608391515?mod=article_inline; Sanger, David E., Nicole Perlroth, and Julian E. Barnes. 2021. "As Understanding of Russian Hacking Grows, So Does Alarm." *The New York Times*. January 2. https://www.nytimes.com/2021/01/02/us/politics/russian-hacking-government.html.

3. Hern, Alex. 2020. "Orion hack Exposed Vast Number of Targets—Impact May Not Be Known for a While." *The Guardian*. December 14. https://www.theguardian.com/world/2020/dec/14/solarwinds-breach-orion-hacked-cyber-espionage.

4. Poulsen, Kevin, Robert McMillan, and Dustin Volz. 2020. "SolarWinds Hack Victims: From Tech Companies to a Hospital and University." *The Wall Street Journal*. December 21. https://www.wsj.com/articles/solarwinds-hack-victims-from-tech-companies-to-a-hospital-and-university-11608548402.

5. Turton, William. 2020. "At Least 200 Victims Identified in Suspected Russian Hacking." Bloomberg. December 19. https://www.bloomberg.com/news/articles/2020-12-19/at-least-200-victims-identified-in-suspected-russian-hacking.

6. Volz, Dustin, and Robert McMillan. 2021. "SolarWinds Hack Breached Justice Department System." *The Wall Street Journal*. January 6. https://www.wsj.com/articles/solarwinds-hack-breached-justice-department-systems-11609958761; Krebs, Brian. 2020. "VMware Flaw a Vector in SolarWinds Breach?" Krebs on Security. December 20. https://krebsonsecurity.com/2020/12/vmware-flaw-a-vector-in-solarwinds-breach/.

7. Perlroth, Nicole, David E. Sanger, and Julian E. Barnes. 2021. "Widely Used Software Company May Be Entry Point for Huge U.S. Hacking." *The New York Times*. January 6. https://www.nytimes.com/2021/01/06/us/politics/russia-cyber-hack.html.

8. Poulsen, Kevin, Robert McMillan, and Dustin Volz. 2020. "SolarWinds Hack Victims: From Tech Companies to a Hospital and University." *The Wall Street Journal*. December 21. https://www.wsj.com/articles/solarwinds-hack-victims-from-tech-companies-to-a-hospital-and-university-11608548402.

9. Mandia, Kevin. 2020. "FireEye Shares Details of Recent Cyber Attack, Actions to Protect Community." FireEye Stories. December 8. https://www.fireeye.com/blog/products-and-services/2020/12/fireeye-shares-details-of-recent-cyber-attack-actions-to-protect-community.html.

10. Ibid.

11. National Cyber Awareness System. 2020. "Advanced Persistent Threat Compromise of Government Agencies, Critical Infrastructure, and Private Sector Organizations." U.S. Cybersecurity and Infrastructure Security Agency. December 17. https://us-cert.cisa.gov/ncas/alerts/aa20-352a.

12. Poulsen, Kevin, Robert McMillan, and Dustin Volz. 2020. "SolarWinds Hack Victims: From Tech Companies to a Hospital and University." *The Wall Street Journal*. December 21. https://www.wsj.com/articles/solarwinds-hack-victims-from-tech-companies-to-a-hospital-and-university-11608548402.

13. Perlroth, Nicole, David E. Sanger, and Julian E. Barnes. 2021. "Widely Used Software Company May Be Entry Point for Huge U.S. Hacking." *The New York Times*. January 6. https://www.nytimes.com/2021/01/06/us/politics/russia-cyber-hack.html.

14. Volz, Dustin. 2017. "U.S. Tech Firm Settles Probe of Russian Work on Defense Project." Reuters. December 11. https://www.reuters.com/article/us-usa-cyber-netcracker/u-s-tech-firm-settles-probe-of-russian-work-on-defense-project-idUSKBN1E52AO.

15. Viswanatha, Aruna, and Del Quentin Wilber. 2017. "Software Firm Settles U.S. Security Probe Over Its Links to Russia." *The Wall Street Journal*. December 11. https://www.wsj.com/articles/software-firm-settles-u-s-security-probe-over-its-links-to-russia-1513004400.

16. Whitman, M., and H. Mattord. 2016. *Management of Information Security*. 5th ed. Boston: Cengage Learning.

17. Cole, E. 2015. "Detect, Contain and Control Cyberthreats: A SANS Whitepaper." SANS. https://www.sans.org/reading-room/whitepapers/analyst/detect-control-cyberthreats-36187.

18. Ibid.

19. Cichonski, P., T. Millar, T. Grance, and K. Scarfone. 2012. "Computer Security Incident Handling Guide: Recommendations of the National Institute of Standards and Technology." NIST Special Publication 800-61 Revision 2. https://csrc.nist.gov/publications/detail/sp/800-61/rev-2/final.

20. U.S. Department of Homeland Security. 2009. "Recommended Practice: Developing an Industrial Control Systems Cybersecurity Incident Response Capability." https://ics-cert.us-cert.gov/sites/default/files/recommended_practices/final-RP_ics_cybersecurity_incident_response_100609.pdf.

21. Advanced Software Products Group. 2017. "The Three States of Digital Data." http://aspg.com/three-states-digital-data/#.Wcn-rtMjFhE.

22. Stallings, W. 2014. "Physical Security Essentials." In *Cyber Security and IT Infrastructure Protection*, J. R. Vacca, ed., 109–134. Waltham, MA: Syngress. .

23. Ibid.

24. Scarfone, K., and P. Mell. 2007. "Guide to Intrusion Detection and Prevention Systems (IDPS): Recommendations of the National Institute of Standards and Technology." NIST Special Publication 800-94. http://nvlpubs.nist.gov/nistpubs/Legacy/SP/nistspecialpublication800-94.pdf.

25. Ibid.

26. Entrust. 2003. "The Concept of Trust in Network Security." https://www.entrust.com/wp-content/uploads/2000/08/trust.pdf.

27. Rous, M. 2013. "Digital Certificate." Tech Target. http://searchsecurity.techtarget.com/definition/digital-certificate.

28. Brecht, Daniel. 2015. "Tales from the Crypt: Hardware vs. Software." InfoSecurity. https://www.infosecurity-magazine.com/magazine-features/tales-crypt-hardware-software/.

29. Carney, J. 2011. "Why Integrate Physical and Logical Security?" Cisco Systems. https://www.cisco.com/c/dam/en_us/solutions/industries/docs/gov/pl-security.pdf.

30. Voldal, D. 2003. "A Practical Methodology for Implementing a Patch Management Process." SANS. https://www.sans.org/reading-room.

31. Ladley, J. 2012. *Data Governance: How to Design, Deploy, and Sustain an Effective Data Governance Program*. Waltham, MA: Elsevier..

32. Dyché, J., and A. Polsky. n.d. "5 Models for Data Stewardship." SANS. https://www.sas.com/content/dam/SAS/en_us/doc/whitepaper1/5-models-for-data-stewardship-106846.pdf.

33. O'Neal, K. n.d. "What Is the Relationship Between Data Architecture and Data Governance?" https://www.firstsanfranciscopartners.com/blog/data-architecture-data-governance-relationship/?cn-reloaded=1.

34. Ladley, J. 2012. *Data Governance: How to Design, Deploy, and Sustain an Effective Data Governance Program*. Waltham, MA: Elsevier.

35. Seismi. n.d. "Metadata vs. Masterdata: Are They the Same Thing?" http://www.seismi.net/metadata-vs-masterdata-what-is-the-difference.

36. Cole, E. 2015. "Detect, Contain and Control Cyberthreats: A SANS Whitepaper." SANS. https://www.sans.org/reading-room/whitepapers/analyst/detect-control-cyberthreats-36187.

37. Ibid.

38. Huntress Labs. n.d. https://huntresslabs.com/index.html.

Chapter 7

1. Capital One. 2019. "Capital One Announces Data Security Incident." Capital One Press Releases. July 29. https://www.capitalone.com/about/newsroom/capital-one-announces-data-security-incident/.

2. CyberInt. 2019. "Report: CyberInt's Take on the Capital One Data Breach." July. https://l.cyberint.com/cyberint-on-capital-one-data-breach.

3. Capital One. 2019. "Capital One Announces Data Security Incident." Capital One Press Releases. July 29. https://www.capitalone.com/about/newsroom/capital-one-announces-data-security-incident/.

4. CyberInt. 2019. "Report: CyberInt's Take on the Capital One Data Breach." July. https://l.cyberint.com/cyberint-on-capital-one-data-breach.

5. McMillan, Robert. 2019. "How the Accused Capital One Hacker Stole Reams of Data from the Cloud." *The Wall Street Journal*. August 4. https://www.wsj.com/articles/how-the-accused-capital-one-hacker-stole-reams-of-data-from-the-cloud-11564911001?mod=article_inline.

6. U.S. Attorney's Office, Western District of Washington. 2019. "Former Seattle Tech Worker Indicted on Federal Charges for Wire Fraud and Computer Data Theft." U.S. Department of Justice. August 28. https://www.justice.gov/usao-wdwa/pr/former-seattle-tech-worker-indicted-federal-charges-wire-fraud-and-computer-data-theft.

7. Benoit, David, Ben Eisen, and AnnaMaria Andriotis. 2019. "Capital One Hack Puts Low-Profile CEO in Spotlight." *The Wall Street Journal*. August 3. https://www.wsj.com/articles/capital-one-hack-puts-low-profile-ceo-in-spotlight-11564837200.

8. Surane, Jennifer, and Lananh Nguyen. 2019. "Capital One Touted the Cloud's Safety as Hacker Was Breaching It." *Bloomberg*. July 30. https://www.bloomberg.com/news/articles/2019-07-30/capital-one-touted-the-cloud-s-safety-as-hacker-was-breaching-it.

9. Benoit, David, Ben Eisen, and AnnaMaria Andriotis. 2019. "Capital One Hack Puts Low-Profile CEO in Spotlight." *The Wall Street Journal*. August 3.

https://www.wsj.com/articles/capital-one-hack-puts-low-profile-ceo-in-spotlight-11564837200.

10. Ibid.

11. Berthelsen, Christian, William Turton, and Jennifer Surane. 2019. "Tipster's Email Led to Arrest in Massive Capital One Breach." *Bloomberg*. July 30. https://www.bloomberg.com/news/articles/2019-07-30/tipster-s-email-led-to-arrest-in-massive-capital-one-data-breach.

12. Andriotis, AnnaMaria, and Rachel Louise Ensign. 2019. "Capital One Cyber Staff Raised Concerns Before Hack." *The Wall Street Journal*. August 15. https://www.wsj.com/articles/capital-one-cyber-staff-raised-concerns-before-hack-11565906781.

13. Brown, Sherrod, Elizabeth Warren, Robert Menendez, Catherine Cortez Masto, and Jack Reed. 2019. "Senate Banking Committee Democrats Demand Capital One Protect Consumers Impacted by Data Breach." Press Office of Sen. Sherrod Brown. September 12. https://www.brown.senate.gov/newsroom/press/release/senate-banking-committee-democrats-demand-capital-one-protect-consumers-impacted-by-data-breach.

14. Ibid.

15. Turton, William, and Jennifer Surane. 2019. "Capital One Breach a Win for Crowdsourced Cybersecurity." *Bloomberg*. August 6. https://www.bloomberg.com/news/articles/2019-08-06/capital-one-hack-poised-to-boost-white-hat-crowdsourcing.

16. U.S. Department of Homeland Security. 2009. "Recommended Practice: Developing an Industrial Control System Cybersecurity Incident Response Capability." https://ics-cert.us-cert.gov/sites/default/files/recommended_practices/final-RP_ics_cybersecurity_incident_response_100609.pdf.

17. Ibid.

18. Deloitte Touche Tohmatsu Limited. 2016. "Cyber Crisis Management: Readiness, Response, and Recovery." https://www2.deloitte.com/content/dam/Deloitte/global/Documents/Risk/gx-cm-cyber-pov.pdf.

19. Bartock, M., J. Cichonski, M. Souppaya, M. Smith, G. Witte, and K. Scarfone. 2016. "Guide for Cybersecurity Event Recovery." NIST Special Publication 800-184. http://nvlpubs.nist.gov/nistpubs/SpecialPublications/NIST.SP.800-184.pdf.

20. Cichonski, P., T. Millar, T. Grance, and K. Scarfone. 2012. *"Computer Security Incident Handling Guide—Recommendations of the National Institute of Standards and Technology."* NIST Special Publication 800-61 Revision 2. https://csrc.nist.gov/publications/detail/sp/800-61/rev-2/final.

21. Deloitte Touche Tohmatsu Limited. 2016. "Cyber Crisis Management: Readiness, Response, and Recovery." https://www2.deloitte.com/global/en/pages/risk/articles/cyber-crisis-management.html.

22. Cichonski, P., T. Millar, T. Grance, and K. Scarfone. 2012. "Computer Security Incident Handling Guide—Recommendations of the National Institute of

Standards and Technology." NIST Special Publication 800-61 Revision 2. https://csrc.nist.gov/publications/detail/sp/800-61/rev-2/final.

23. Ibid.

24. Cichonski, P., T. Millar, T. Grance, and K. Scarfone. 2012. *"Computer Security Incident Handling Guide—Recommendations of the National Institute of Standards and Technology." NIST Special Publication 800-61 Revision 2.* https:// csrc.nist.gov/publications/detail/sp/800-61/rev-2/final.

25. Deloitte Touche Tohmatsu Limited. 2016. "Cyber Crisis Management: Readiness, Response, and Recovery." https://www2.deloitte.com/global/en/pages/risk/ articles/cyber-crisis-management.html.

26. Williams, Tom. 2017. "Factors to Consider When Planning Cyber Table Top Exercises." Context. https://www.contextis.com/en/blog/planning-cyber-table-top-exercises.

27. Bailey, Tucker, James Kaplan, and Allen Weinberg. 2012. "Playing War Games to Prepare for a Cyberattack." McKinsey. https://www.mckinsey.com/business-functions/mckinsey-digital/our-insights/playing-war-games-to-prepare-for-a-cyberattack.

28. AlienVault. n.d. "Insider's Guide to Incident Response: Expert Tips." https:// www.alienvault.com/resource-center/ebook/insider-guide-to-incident-response.

29. Deloitte Touche Tohmatsu Limited. 2016. "Cyber Crisis Management: Readiness, Response, and Recovery." https://www2.deloitte.com/global/en/pages/risk/ articles/cyber-crisis-management.html.

30. Drinkwater, D., and K. Zurkus. "Red Team Versus Blue Team: How to Run an Effective Simulation." CSO. https://www.csoonline.com/article/2122440/ disaster-recovery/emergency-preparedness-red-team-versus-blue-team-how-to-run-an-effective-simulation.html.

31. Cichonski, P., T. Millar, T. Grance, and K. Scarfone. 2012. "Computer Security Incident Handling Guide—Recommendations of the National Institute of Standards and Technology." NIST Special Publication 800-61 Revision 2. https://csrc.nist.gov/publications/detail/sp/800-61/rev-2/final.

32. Ibid.

33. Ibid.

34. Kral, P. 2012. "The Incident Handler's Handbook." SANS. https://www.sans.org/ reading-room/whitepapers/incident/incident-handlers-handbook-33901.

35. U.S. Department of Homeland Security. 2009. "Recommended Practice: Developing an Industrial Control Systems Cybersecurity Incident Response Capability." https:// ics-cert.us-cert.gov/sites/default/files/recommended_practices/final-RP_ics_ cybersecurity_incident_response_100609.pdf.

36. Cichonski, P., T. Millar, T. Grance, and K. Scarfone. 2012. "Computer Security Incident Handling Guide—Recommendations of the National Institute of Standards and Technology." NIST Special Publication 800-61 Revision 2. https://csrc.nist.gov/publications/detail/sp/800-61/rev-2/final.

37. MIT Technology Review Insights. 2016. "Crisis Communication After an Attack." MIT Technology Review. https://www.technologyreview.com/s/601292/crisis-communication-after-an-attack/.

38. Lunenberg. F. 2010. "Formal Communication Channels: Upward, Downward, Horizontal, and External." https://pdfs.semanticscholar.org/cb0e/c6f253095fa016de05f882ecf4385f3070e6.pdf.

39. Ibid.

40. Cichonski, P., T. Millar, T. Grance, and K. Scarfone. 2012. *"Computer Security Incident Handling Guide—Recommendations of the National Institute of Standards and Technology."* NIST Special Publication 800-61 Revision 2. https://csrc.nist.gov/publications/detail/sp/800-61/rev-2/final.

41. Deloitte Touche Tohmatsu Limited. 2016. *"Cyber Crisis Management: Readiness, Response, and Recovery."* https://www2.deloitte.com/global/en/pages/risk/articles/cyber-crisis-management.html

42. Kral, P. 2012. "The Incident Handlers Handbook." SANS. https://www.sans.org/reading-room/whitepapers/incident/incident-handlers-handbook-33901.

43. Cichonski, P., T. Millar, T. Grance, and K. Scarfone. 2012. *"Computer Security Incident Handling Guide—Recommendations of the National Institute of Standards and Technology."* NIST Special Publication 800-61 Revision 2. https://csrc.nist.gov/publications/detail/sp/800-61/rev-2/final.

44. Bartock, M., J. Cichonski, M. Souppaya, M. Smith, G. Witte, and K. Scarfone. 2016. "Guide for Cybersecurity Event Recovery." NIST Special Publication 800-184. http://nvlpubs.nist.gov/nistpubs/SpecialPublications/NIST.SP.800-184.pdf.

45. Kral, P. 2012. "The Incident Handlers Handbook." SANS. https://www.sans.org/reading-room/whitepapers/incident/incident-handlers-handbook-33901.

46. Bartock, M., J. Cichonski, M. Souppaya, M. Smith, G. Witte, and K. Scarfone. 2016. "Guide for Cybersecurity Event Recovery." NIST Special Publication 800-184. http://nvlpubs.nist.gov/nistpubs/SpecialPublications/NIST.SP.800-184.pdf.

47. Cichonski, P., T. Millar, T. Grance, and K. Scarfone. 2012. "Computer Security Incident Handling Guide—Recommendations of the National Institute of Standards and Technology." NIST Special Publication 800-61 Revision 2. https://csrc.nist.gov/publications/detail/sp/800-61/rev-2/final.

48. Virginia Polytechnic Institute and State University. n.d. "Virginia Tech Guide for Cyber Security Incident Response." https://security.vt.edu/content/dam/security_vt_edu/downloads/incident_response.pdf.

49. Bartock, M., J. Cichonski, M. Souppaya, M. Smith, G. Witte, and K. Scarfone. 2016. "Guide for Cybersecurity Event Recovery." NIST Special Publication 800-184. http://nvlpubs.nist.gov/nistpubs/SpecialPublications/NIST.SP.800-184.pdf.

50. Cichonski, P., T. Millar, T. Grance, and K. Scarfone. 2012. "Computer Security Incident Handling Guide—Recommendations of the National Institute of

Standards and Technology." NIST Special Publication 800-61 Revision 2. https://csrc.nist.gov/publications/detail/sp/800-61/rev-2/final.

51. Ibid.
52. Ibid.
53. Sasso, Brendan. 2012. "Obama Takes Part in Cyberattack Exercise." The Hill. June 5. https://thehill.com/policy/technology/231011-obama-participates-in-cyberattack-exercise.

Chapter 8

1. Ralph, Oliver, and Robert Armstrong. 2019. "Mondelez Sues Zurich in Test for Cyber Hack Insurance." *The Financial Times*. January 9. https://www.ft.com/content/8db7251c-1411-11e9-a581-4ff78404524e.

2. Tressler LLP. 2019. "Illinois Court to Determine if NotPetya Malware Is Excluded as War Under Insurance Policy." Tressler Privacy Risk Report. January 15. https://privacyriskreport.com/illinois-court-to-determine-if-notpetya-malware-is-excluded-as-war-under-insurance-policy/.

3. Mondelez International, Inc. v. Zurich American Insurance Company. 2018. "Mondelez v. Zurich Complaint." Circuit Court of Illinois, Cook County Law Division. October 10. https://www.databreachninja.com/wp-content/uploads/sites/63/2019/01/MONDELEZ-INTERNATIONAL-INC-Plaintiff-v-ZURICH-AMERICAN-INSURANCE-COMPANY-Defenda.pdf.

4. Mondelez International, Inc. v. Zurich American Insurance Company. 2018. "Civil Action Cover Sheet: Mondelez v. Zurich." Clerk of the Circuit Court of Cook County, Illinois. October 10. https://assets.documentcloud.org/documents/5759256/397265756-Mondelez-Zurich.pdf.

5. Corcoran, Brian. 2019. "What Mondelez v. Zurich May Reveal About Cyber Insurance in the Age of Digital Conflict." *Lawfare* (blog). March 8. https://www.lawfareblog.com/what-mondelez-v-zurich-may-reveal-about-cyber-insurance-age-digital-conflict.

6. Tressler LLP. 2019. "Illinois Court to Determine if NotPetya Malware Is Excluded as War Under Insurance Policy." Tressler Privacy Risk Report. January 15. https://privacyriskreport.com/illinois-court-to-determine-if-notpetya-malware-is-excluded-as-war-under-insurance-policy/.

7. Ralph, Oliver, and Robert Armstrong. 2019. "Mondelez Sues Zurich in Test for Cyber Hack Insurance." *The Financial Times*. January 9. https://www.ft.com/content/8db7251c-1411-11e9-a581-4ff78404524e.

8. Gangar, A. 2015. "Benefits of Adopting the NIST Cybersecurity Framework." LinkedIn. https://www.linkedin.com/pulse/benefits-adopting-nist-cybersecurity-framework-ashish-gangar/.

9. Summit Consulting Group. 2015. "Challenges When Implementing a Strategy." https://summitconsultinggroupllc.com/strategy-definition/.

10. U.S. Department of Defense. 2015. "Cyber Strategy, 2015." https://archive.defense.gov/home/features/2015/0415_cyber-strategy/final_2015_dod_cyber_strategy_for_web.pdf.